# International HIPAA, Privacy, and Security Law Considerations

RACHEL V. ROSE AND LANCE H. ROSE

AMERICAN BAR ASSOCIATION
Health Law Section

Cover design by Elizabeth Kulak/ABA Design



Printed in the United States of America.

28 27 26 25 24 5 4 3 2 1

A catalog record for this book is available from the Library of Congress.

ISBN 978-1-63905-183-0

# CONTENTS

# INTRODUCTION

Are you familiar with the 1988 General Motors' Oldsmobile marketing slogan "this is not your father's Oldsmobile"—where the company paired celebrities like William Shatner and Ringo Starr with their adult children to illustrate the new generation of cars to capture a new customer base?

This same concept applies to this book, as it builds upon the still relevant *What Are International HIPAA Considerations?* while also addressing the new generation of cybersecurity laws, compliance requirements, and threats, which need to be considered in conjunction with the Health Insurance Portability and Accountability Act of 1996 (HIPAA)—a law that celebrated its 25th anniversary in August 2021 and continues to evolve.

International cybercriminals have become more brazen, as attacks in 2021 and 2022 were aimed at children's hospitals—Boston's Children's Hospital[1] and the Hospital for Sick Children in Toronto, Canada.[2] As the Federal Bureau of Investigation (FBI) noted, "[w]e got a report from one of our intelligence partners indicating Boston Children's was about to be targeted. And, understanding the urgency of the situation, the cyber squad in our Boston Field Office raced to notify the hospital."[3] The attack was thwarted and both the kids and the network were protected.

---

1. Mike Miliard, *Boston Children's Hospital Was Target of Cyberattack Thwarted by FBI*, Healthcare IT News (June 2, 2022), https://www.healthcareitnews.com/news/boston-childrens-hospital-was-target-cyberattack-thwarted-fbi.

2. James Coker, *Cyber-Incident Causes System Failures at Canadian Children's Hospital*, Infosecurity Mag. (Dec. 21, 2022), https://www.infosecurity-magazine.com/news/cyber-incident-failure-children/.

3. Christopher Wray, Director, Federal Bureau of Investigations, *Director's Remarks to the Boston Conference on Cyber Security 2022* (June 1, 2022), https://www.fbi.gov/news/speeches/directors-remarks-to-boston-conference-on-cyber-security-2022?utm_campaign=email-Immediate&utm_medium=email&utm_source=executive-speeches&utm_content=%5B1421169%5D-%2Fnews%2Fspeeches%2Fdirectors-remarks-to-boston-conference-on-cyber-security-2022.

Actions like those perpetrated on children's hospitals, as well as other infrastructure considerations, such as the Colonial Pipeline prompted Executive Order 14028, Improving the Nation's Cybersecurity, which called for the public sector and the private sector to improve the prevention, detection, and correction of cyber risks and events.[4] Government agencies, including the U.S. Department of Justice acted and implemented cyber-fraud and other cybersecurity enforcement initiatives.[5]

As this book is headed to publication, cybersecurity risks continue to escalate. As a *Harvard Business Review* article, "The Cybersecurity Risks of an Escalating Russia-Ukraine Conflict," states, "[t]he implications for business of conflict in Ukraine—whether conventional, cyber, or hybrid—will be felt far beyond the region's borders."[6] Now more than ever, healthcare industry participants—whether covered entities, business associates, or subcontractors—should utilize resources such as those set forth by the U.S. Department of Health and Human Services (HHS), Health Sector Cybersecurity Coordination (HC3).[7]

*International HIPAA, Privacy, and Security Law Considerations* is a valuable resource, as health expenditures as a percentage of gross domestic product (GDP) continue to grow, reaching significant levels in various countries (for example, the United States spends nearly 17 percent of GDP on healthcare, whereas the United Kingdom spends approximately 10.2 percent).[8] The book addresses health systems that continue to outsource information technology services (IT services),[9] and the escalat-

4. *Executive Order on Improving the Nation's Cybersecurity*, The White House (May 12, 2021), https://www.whitehouse.gov/briefing-room/presidential-actions/2021/05/12/executive-order-on-improving-the-nations-cybersecurity/.

5. Press Release, U.S. Dep't of Just., Deputy Attorney General Lisa O. Monaco Announces New Civil Cyber-Fraud Initiative (Oct. 6, 2021), https://www.justice.gov/opa/pr/deputy-attorney-general-lisa-o-monaco-announces-new-civil-cyber-fraud-initiative.

6. Paul R. Kolbe, Maria Robson-Morrow & Lauren Zabierek, *The Cybersecurity Risks of an Escalating Russia-Ukraine Conflict*, Harvard Bus. Rev. (updated Feb. 24, 2022), https://hbr.org/2022/02/the-cybersecurity-risks-of-an-escalating-russia-ukraine-conflict.

7. *Health Sector Cybersecurity Coordinator (HC3)*, U.S. Dep't of Health & Hum. Servs., https://www.hhs.gov/about/agencies/asa/ocio/hc3/index.html (last updated Dec. 12, 2023).

8. *Health Expenditure as a Percentage of Gross Domestic Product (GDP) in Selected Countries in 2022*, Statistica, https://www.statista.com/statistics/268826/health-expenditure-as-gdp-percentage-in-oecd-countries/ (last visited May 15, 2024).

9. Kristy Boldt, *Why Most Hospitals Outsource IT & How to Do Healthcare IT Outsourcing Right*, Medsphere (Feb. 14, 2020), https://www.medsphere.com/blog/hospitals

ing threats by malicious cybercriminals toward healthcare organizations and patient safety, as well as enforcement and compliance initiatives by various governments.[10] Regardless of your role as a lawyer, consultant, or healthcare industry participant, there is something for everyone in this book.

---

-are-outsourcing-it-and-how/ (indicating that according to Black Book Research, approximately 75 percent of health systems with 300 or more beds and 81 percent of health systems with fewer than 300 beds outsource IT services).

10. *Alert (AA20-302A)—Ransomware Activity Targeting the Healthcare and Public Health Sector*, Cybersecurity & Infrastructure Security Agency, https://us-cert.cisa.gov/ncas/alerts/aa20-302a (last revised Nov. 2, 2020).

# ABOUT THE AUTHORS

**Rachel V. Rose**, JD, MBA, advises and represents clients in compliance, transactional, litigation, and government enforcement matters involving healthcare, cybersecurity, securities, False Claims Act and Dodd-Frank matters. Ms. Rose is also an affiliated member with the Baylor College of Medicine's Center for Medical Ethics and Health Policy, where she teaches bioethics. She is often quoted as an expert.

Ms. Rose is licensed in Texas and is a Fellow of the Federal Bar Association. Currently, she is a director on the Federal Bar Association's National Board, is a member of and the immediate past chair of the Federal Bar Association's Government Relations Committee, and is an Advisory Board member of the Federal Bar Association's *Qui Tam* Section. Ms. Rose is the co-editor of the American Health Lawyers Association's *Enterprise Risk Management Handbook for Healthcare Entities* (second edition), as well as a co-author of the ABA's books *The ABCs of ACOs* and *What Are International HIPAA Considerations?* She is extensively published and presents on a variety of matters related to her practice.

She has been named consecutively to the Texas Bar College, the National Women Trial Lawyers Association's Top 25, *Houstonia Magazine*'s Top Lawyers (healthcare), the National Trial Lawyers Association's Top 100, as well as 1st Healthcare Compliance's 2019 Top Presenter. Ms. Rose co-represented Relator Dr. Shawn Lawler in the False Claims Act lawsuit, which resulted in the first settlement obtained by the U.S. Department of Justice under its Cyber-Fraud Initiative.[11]

11. Press Release, U.S. Dep't of Just., Medical Services Contractor Pays $930,000 to Settle False Claims Act Allegations Relating to Medical Services Contracts as State Department and Air Force Facilities in Iraq and Afghanistan (Mar. 8, 2022), https://www.justice.gov/opa/pr/medical-services-contractor-pays-930000-settle-false-claims-act-allegations-relating-medical.

**Lance H. Rose**, MHA, MS, LFACHE, is a retired hospital chief executive officer with more than 40 years of healthcare experience. Mr. Rose has served on numerous boards, including the American Hospital Association's Regional Policy Board and BlueCross BlueShield. He also taught as an adjunct professor at The Pennsylvania State University and has authored and co-authored a variety of articles and books, including *What Are International HIPAA Considerations?*

# PART I

## Laying the Foundation

# CHAPTER 1

# A Framework for Digesting Cybersecurity

"How do you eat an elephant? One bite at a time."

—Unknown

The focus of this chapter is to provide an incremental approach to cybersecurity, whether a program is just being implemented or continues to evolve, these fundamental suggestions can assist with the implementation of risk management and related internal programs, which contribute to an entity's goal of cultivating a culture of compliance.

## Suggested Approaches to Cybersecurity

Cybersecurity can be overwhelming. The laws and standards, as well as the technical, administrative, and physical safeguards are plentiful. So, what's the best way to approach the topic? First, consider the general tips found in *Health Care Compliance Program Tips: The Seven Fundamental Elements of an Effective Compliance Program,* which was published by the U.S. Department of Health and Human Services—Office of the Inspector General (HHS-OIG).[1] The elements are as follows:

1. Implementing written policies, procedures, and standards of conduct.
2. Designating a compliance officer and a compliance committee.
3. Conducting effective training and education.
4. Developing effective lines of communication.
5. Conducting internal monitoring and auditing.
6. Enforcing standards through well-publicized disciplinary guidelines.
7. Responding promptly to detected offenses and undertaking corrective action.

1. *See* https://oig.hhs.gov/documents/provider-compliance-training/945/Compliance101tips508.pdf (last visited Jan. 8, 2023).

Once these seven pillars for a general framework have been established, HHS-OIG suggests that organizations make compliance an immediate priority, appreciate risk areas, manage financial and contractor/client relationships, and when in doubt seek advice from a knowledgeable source.[2] Although HHS-OIG is primarily tasked with fraud, waste, and abuse, these concepts also apply to complying with the Health Insurance Portability and Accountability Act of 1996 (HIPAA),[3] the Health Information Technology for Economic and Clinical Health Act (HITECH Act)[4] and related amendments,[5] state laws (e.g., California Consumer Protection Act (CCPA),[6] California Confidentiality of Medical Information Act (CMIA),[7] and Texas H.B. 300[8]), and international laws (e.g., European Union's Data Protection Regulation (GDPR),[9] Philippines' The Data Privacy Act of 2012 (DPA)[10]). This is where ascertaining the entity's corporate culture intersects with its cybersecurity compliance program and enterprise risk management.

As set forth in *NISTIR 8286 Integrating Cybersecurity and Enterprise Risk Management (ERM),*

> [t]he effect of uncertainty on *enterprise* mission and business objectives may then be considered an "enterprise risk" that

---

2. *Id.*

3. Pub. L. No. 104-191 (Aug. 21, 1996).

4. Pub. L. No. 111-5 (Feb. 17, 2009).

5. Pub. L. No. 116-321 (Jan. 5, 2021).

6. Title 1.81.5 Cal. Civ. Code, as amended by the California Privacy Rights Act of 2020 (CPRA), Cal. Civ. Code §§ 1798.150, *et seq.* (effective Jan. 1, 2023) (substantially amending and highlighting the CCPA requirements, more closely aligning it with the European Union's General Data Protection Regulation (EU 2016/679)).

7. Cal. Civ. Code §§ 56, *et seq.*, as amended by CA SB 1419 (changing California law to allow physicians additional time to evaluate potentially life-changing test results before releasing them to the patient, adding legal protections for very sensitive data such as teen mental health and reproductive data, and clarifying that clinical notes are part of the patient's medical record, among other items).

8. Amending four areas of Texas legislation—the Texas Health and Safety Code (chapters 181 and 182), the Texas Business and Commerce Code (chapter 531), and the Texas Insurance Code (chapter 602)—and requiring stricter privacy protections for health information than HIPAA.

9. General Data Protection Regulation (EU 2016/679).

10. Republic Act No. 10173 (effective Sept. 8, 2012) (governing law on data privacy in the Philippines).

must be similarly managed. An *enterprise* is an organization that exists at the top level of a hierarchy with unique risk management responsibilities. Managing risks at that level is known as enterprise risk management (ERM) and calls for understanding the core risks that an enterprise faces, determining how best to address those risks, and ensuring that the necessary actions are taken. In the Federal Government, ERM is considered "an effective agency-wide approach to addressing the full spectrum of the organization's significant risks by understanding the combined impact of risks as an interrelated portfolio rather than addressing risks only within silos.[11]

In terms of ERM, the first step is to create an "ERM Playbook" that has the following components:

1. Identify the context (i.e., management strategy, risk tolerance, mission, corporate culture).
2. Conduct a risk assessment (aka risk analysis in HIPAA).
   a. Identify the risks within the framework of NIST, HIPAA, and ISO's technical, administrative, and physical safeguards; characterize threat sources; identify potential threat events; and evaluate vulnerabilities that may be exploited and lead to a breach (or in healthcare, even a patient death).
   b. Analyze the risks, the likelihood, and impact.
   c. Prioritize risks.
   d. Calculate exposure.
   e. Plan and execute response strategies.
2. Monitor, evaluate, and adjust.

Table 1.1 is a great resource for identifying similarities and differences between different NIST enterprise risk resources.

11. *See* Kevin Stine et al., *NISTIR 8286 Integrating Cybersecurity and Enterprise Risk Management (ERM)*, U.S. Dep't of Com. (Oct. 2020), https://nvlpubs.nist.gov/nistpubs/ir/2020/NIST.IR.8286.pdf.

**Table 1.1** Similarities among Selected ERM and Risk Management Documents

| ERM Playbook | ISO 31000: 2018 | OMB A-123 | GAO Green Book | NIST Risk Managemnet Documents: SP 800-30 Rev. 1 | SP 800-37 Rev. 2 | SP 800-39 |
|---|---|---|---|---|---|---|
| Identify the Context | Establish External Context (5.3.2), Establish Internal Context (5.3.3) | Establish Context | Define objectives and risk tolerances (6.01) | Preparing for the Risk Assessment (3.1) | Prepare (3.1) (P-2: Risk Management Strategy) | Framing Risk (3.1) |
| | Risk Assessment: Risk Identification (5.4.2) | Idetify Risks | Indetification of Risks (7.02) | Task 2-1: Identify and characterize threat sources of concern (3.2), Task 2-2: Identify potential threat events threat sources (3.2), Task 2-3: Identify vulnerabiliies/predispositioned conditions (3.2) | Prepare (3.1), Task P-3, Task P-14 Output: Rish Assessment Report | |
| Analyze the Risks | Risk Analysis (5.4.3) | Analyze and Evaluate | Analysis of Risks (7.05) | Task 2-5: Determine the adverse events (3.2), Task 2-4: Determine the likelihood (3.2), Task 2-6: Determine the risk to the organication (3.2) Risk Assessment Report (Appendix K) | | Assessing Risk (3.2) SP800-30 |
| Assess Likelihood | Calculate Level of Risk | | Management estimates the significance of a risk and considers the magnitude of impact, likelihood of occurrence and nature of the risk | | | |
| Assess Impact | | | | | | |
| Prioritize Risks | | | | | | |
| Plan and Execute Response Strategies | | Development Alternatives | Response to Risks (7.08) | Task 3-1: Communicate Risk Assessment Results Task 3-2: Share Risk-Related Information (3.3) Also See 800-37 Rev. 2 See 800-39 | R-3: Risk Response | Responding to Risk (3.3) |
| | Risk Treatment (5.5) | Respond to Risks | | | Categorize (3.2) (C-2, C-3), Select (3.3) (S-1, S-2, S-3), and implement (3.4) (I1.I2), Authorize (3.6) (R-4), Task A-6 Plan of Action and Milestones | |
| Monitor, Evaluate, and Adjust | Monitoring and review (5.6) | Monitor and Review | Identification of Change (9.02)<br>Analysis of and Response to Change (9.04) | Task 4-1: Conduct ongoing monitoring of the risk factors (3.4) Task 4-2: Update Risk Assessment | Monitor (3.7) (M-1, M-2, M-3, M-6) | Monitoring Risk (3.4) |

https://nvlpubs.nist.gov/nistpubs/ir/2020/NIST.IR.8286.pdf

A risk assessment (or HIPAA risk analysis[12]) "is the first step in identifying and implementing safeguards that comply with and carry out the standards and implementation specifications."[13] In sum, a qualified, external third party should conduct a foundational risk analysis, in addition to conducting an internal assessment on a continual basis to ensure that the identified gaps are rectified and that new threats are detected. Additionally, it is ill-advised for a company to dictate that an auditor read the company's previous risk analyses/risk assessments and other related documents before the auditor conducts an audit. Doing so could create a bias. From here, let's delve into how standards such as NIST and ISO impact audits, compliance, legal proceedings, and government enforcement actions.

## The Role of Standards in Audits, Compliance, Legal Proceedings, and Government Enforcement Actions

Those who are involved in government contracting or work for the U.S. government may already be aware of the National Institute of Standards and Technology (NIST) standards and the International Organization for Standardization (ISO) standards.[14] In today's world, where the number of cyberattacks continues to rise and a plethora of state, federal, and international laws continues to emerge in relation to privacy and security, it is imperative to understand the role that NIST and ISO standards play.

As for law enforcement observations in the United States and abroad—what are they seeing? On March 3, 2022, HHS Cybersecurity Program—Office of Information Security published *Health Sector Cybersecurity: 2021 Retrospective and 2022 Look Ahead,* a report that highlighted that cybercriminals and nation-states attacking the healthcare sector is not new, that ransomware and data breaches remain prevalent, and that threats and threat actors continue to evolve and become more

12. 45 C.F.R. § 164.308(a)(1)(ii)(A).

13. *Guidance on Risk Analysis,* U.S. Dep't of Health & Hum. Servs., https://www.hhs.gov/hipaa/for-professionals/security/guidance/guidance-risk-analysis/index.html (last updated July 22, 2019).

14. *See* https://www.iso.org/standards-catalogue/browse-by-ics.html (last visited Mar. 5, 2022).

sophisticated.[15] The Federal Bureau of Investigation (FBI), which is the lead federal agency investigating cyberattacks, indicated, "[m]alicious cyber activity threatens the public's safety and our national and economic security."[16]

## *Initiatives Involving NIST*

Founded in 1901, NIST falls under the umbrella of the U.S. Department of Commerce. "Today, NIST measurements support the smallest of technologies to the largest and most complex of human-made creations—from nanoscale devices so tiny that tens of thousands can fit on the end of a single human hair up to the earthquake-resistant skyscrapers and global communication networks."[17] NIST issues publications typically known as NIST Special Publications, and also publishes the Federal Information Processing Standards (FIPS). Although NIST and FIPS publications are standards, express compliance with these publications and standards may be required in the text of laws and regulations.

One example of NIST being expressly stated in a law that is relevant to the healthcare sector and includes covered entities, business associates, and subcontractors alike is H.R. 7898, which became Pub. L. 116-321 (Jan. 5, 2021). For example, Pub. L. 116-321 amends the HITECH Act and provides an additional type of "safe harbor" in the event of an HHS-OCR investigation if "recognized security practices" were in place.

Recognized security practices are the standards, guidelines, best practices, methodologies, procedures, and processes developed under section 2(c)(15) of the National Institute of Standards and Technology Act, the approaches promulgated under section 405(d) of the Cybersecurity Act of 2015, and other programs and processes that address cybersecurity and that are developed, recognized, or promulgated through regulations under other statutory authorities. Such practices are determined by the covered entity or business associate, consistent with the HIPAA Security

---

15. *See* U.S. Dep't of Health & Hum. Servs, Health Sector Cybersecurity: 2021 Retrospective and 2022 Look Ahead 3 (Mar. 3, 2022), https://www.hhs.gov/sites/default/files/2021-retrospective-and-2022-look-ahead-tlpwhite.pdf.

16. *The Cyber Threat*, FBI, https://www.fbi.gov/investigate/cyber (last visited Mar. 5, 2022).

17. *See* https://www.nist.gov/about-nist (last visited Mar. 5, 2022).

Rule (part 160 of title 45 Code of Federal Regulations and subparts A and C of part 164 of such title).

Pub. L. 116-132(a)(1)–(3) expressly states that having recognized security practices in place may:

> (1) mitigate fines under section 1176 of the Social Security Act (as amended by section 13410);
>
> (2) result in the early, favorable termination of an audit under section 13411; and
>
> (3) mitigate the remedies that would otherwise be agreed to in any agreement with respect to resolving potential violations of the HIPAA Security rule (part 160 of title 45 Code of Federal Regulations and subparts A and C of part 164 of such title) between the covered entity or business associate and the Department of Health and Human Services.

If a person is seeking to mitigate the risk of a fine and other correctives actions and legal proceedings from HHS-OCR and develop a comprehensive cybersecurity compliance program, then it is prudent to utilize NIST domestically and ISO when appropriate—whether prescribed by law or whether the person is conducting business outside of the United States.

## *Appreciating the ISO Standards*

An independent, nongovernmental international organization, ISO was established in 1946 and is based in Switzerland.[18] It includes "167 national standards bodies" within its membership. Like NIST, ISO standards are widely accepted after being created by consensus from input by experts from both international governments and the private sector. As stated on its website, ISO suggests, "[t]hink[ing] of them [ISO standards] as a formula that describes the best way of doing something."[19] Like NIST, ISO has various publications. ISO 27001 and ISO 27002 are two of the cornerstone publications, which should be utilized both in compliance

18. *See* https://www.iso.org/about-us.html (last visited Mar. 5, 2022).
19. *See* https://www.iso.org/standards.html (last visited Mar. 5, 2022).

efforts, as well as in cybersecurity audits to assess technical, administrative, and physical safeguards.[20]

The information security management standard ISO 27001 and the related code of practice ISO 27002 were last updated nearly a decade ago.[21] Here are some of the key take-aways:

ISO 27002:2022 lists 93 controls rather than ISO 27002:2013's 114.

- These controls are grouped into 4 "themes" rather than 14 clauses. They are:
  - People (8 controls)
  - Organizational (37 controls)
  - Technological (34 controls)
  - Physical (14 controls)
- The completely new controls are:
  - Threat intelligence
  - Information security for use of cloud services
  - ICT readiness for business continuity
  - Physical security monitoring
  - Configuration management
  - Information deletion
  - Data masking
  - Data leakage prevention
  - Monitoring activities
  - Web filtering
  - Secure coding
- The controls now also have five types of "attribute[s]" to make them easier to categorize:
  - Control type (preventive, detective, corrective)
  - Information security properties (confidentiality, integrity, availability)
  - Cybersecurity concepts (identify, protect, detect, respond, recover)
  - Operational capabilities (governance, asset management, etc.)

---

20. *See* https://www.itgovernance.co.uk/iso27001-and-iso27002-2022-updates (last visited Mar. 5, 2022).

21. *Id.*

- Security domains (governance and ecosystem, protection, defense, resilience)[22]

ISO standards are critical for persons that fall under the umbrella of the European Union's GDPR, which repealed Data Protection Directive 95/46/EC because of the aim of protecting the confidentiality, integrity, and availability of personal data.[23]

The best practice is to have a crosswalk map that includes the HIPAA Security Rule and maps to both NIST and ISO standards.[24] As the reader advances through this book, these standards should be considered.

## The Intersection between Privacy and Security

Two basic terms utilized in everyday conversation: privacy and security. What do they mean in the context of cybersecurity? Once again, let's turn to NIST and ISO, which defines these two words as follows:

**Privacy**

> NIST SP 800-130: "[a]ssurance that the confidentiality of, and access to, certain information about an entity [or an individual] is protected. The right of a party to maintain control over and confidentiality of information about itself [or themselves]."[25]
>
> ISO/IEC 2382: "freedom from intrusion into the private life or affairs of an individual when that intrusion results from undue or illegal gathering and use of data about that individual."[26]

---

22. *Id.*

23. *See* https://gdpr.eu (last visited Mar. 5, 2022).

24. *See* https://reciprocity.com/blog/how-to-map-hipaa-to-iso-27001/ (Sept. 21, 2021); *see also HIPAA Security Rule Crosswalk to NIST Cybersecurity Framework*, U.S. Dep't of Health & Hum. Servs. https://www.hhs.gov/guidance/document/hipaa-security-rule-crosswalk-nist-cybersecurity-framework (last visited June 1, 2024).

25. NIST SP 800-130, *Privacy*, https://csrc.nist.gov/glossary/term/privacy (last visited Jan. 3, 2023).

26. ISO/IEC 2382, *Privacy*, https://www.iso.org/obp/ui#iso:std:iso-iec:2382:ed-1:v2:en (last visited Jan. 3, 2023).

**Security**

> NIST SP 800-66, Rev. 1: "[p]rotecting information and information systems from unauthorized access, use, disclosure, disruption, modification, or destruction in order to provide—(A) integrity, which means guarding against improper information modification or destruction, and includes ensuring information non-repudiation and authenticity; (B) confidentiality, which means preserving authorized restrictions on access and disclosure, including means for protecting personal privacy and proprietary information; and (C) availability, which means ensuring timely and reliable access to and use of information."[27]
>
> ISO/IEC/IEEE 15288:2015: "[p]rotection against intentional subversion or forced failure. A composite of four attributes—confidentiality, integrity, availability, and accountability—plus aspects of a fifth, usability, all of which have the related issue of their assurance."[28]

To keep information private, appropriate security measures must be in place. HIPAA has a separate Privacy Rule and Security Rule; however, the end goal is the same for each—providing the patients timely access to their protected health information and keeping it secure by utilizing appropriate safeguards to ensure the confidentiality, integrity, and availability of the information. In sum, the safest way to approach cybersecurity is to assess both the privacy requirements and the security requirements of HIPAA[29] and other laws such as GDPR.[30]

---

27. NIST SP 800-66, Rev. 1, *Security*, https://csrc.nist.gov/glossary/term/security (last visited Jan. 3, 2023).

28. ISO/IEC/IEEE 15288:2015, *Security*, https://www.govinfo.gov/content/pkg/GOVPUB-C13-c25c4bc1a2f4ce59b0e727473363724e/pdf/GOVPUB-C13-c25c4bc1a2f4ce59b0e727473363724e.pdf.

29. HHS-OCR, *Health Information Privacy*, https://www.hhs.gov/hipaa/index.html (last visited Jan. 3, 2023).

30. Ben Wolford, *What Is GDPR, the EU's New Data Protection Law?*, GDPR EU, https://gdpr.eu/what-is-gdpr/ (last visited Jan. 3, 2023).

# CHAPTER 2

# Risk

"Life is all about taking risks. If you never take risks, then you'll never know what you're capable of."[1]

Have you ever heard of the board game *Risk*? The endgame is simple: "players aim to conquer their enemies' territories by building an army, moving their troops in, and engaging in battle. Depending on the 'roll of the dice,' a player will either defeat the enemy or be defeated."[2] Stated another way, Risk = Probability × Severity. But why is it relevant to cybersecurity and how does it come into play in risk assessments?

## What Is Risk?

As set forth in NIST SP 800-38C, "[t]he level or potential impact on an organization's operations (including mission, functions, image, or reputation), organization assets, or individuals of a threat or a given likelihood of that threat occurring."[3] In layman's terms, according to *Merriam Webster*, "security risk" is defined as "someone who could damage an organization by giving information to an enemy or competitor."[4] The best way to manage cyber risk is through a comprehensive risk management program.

For healthcare industry participants, a fundamental risk that cannot be overlooked is adverse patient outcomes, including death. The American Hospital Association has been promoting cybersecurity for patient

---

1. https://morningthoughts843.blog/2023/07/07/take-a-risk/.

2. Hasbro, *Risk: The Game of Strategic Conquest*, https://shop.hasbro.com/en-us/product/risk-game/2C7C6F52-5056-9047-F5DD-EB8AC273BA4C# (last visited Jan. 4, 2024).

3. NIST, *Definition of Risk* (from NIST SP 800-38C, Recommendation for Block Cipher Modes of Operation: the CCM Mode for Authentication and Confidentiality), https://csrc.nist.gov/glossary/term/risk#:~:text=NIST%20SP%20800%2D38C%20under,likelihood%20of%20that%20threat%20occurring (last visited Jan. 4, 2024).

4. Merriam Webster, *Security Risk*, https://www.merriam-webster.com/dictionary/security%20risk#:~:text=noun,be%20deemed%20a%20security%20risk (last visited Apr. 27, 2023).

safety since at least November 2022 and they are right. Whether it is the new U.S. Food and Drug Administration's cybersecurity requirements for medical devices or Health and Human Services (HHS) HHS 405(d) *HICP 2023 Edition* to help persons managing threats, the end game is to strengthen an organization's posture against cyber threats in order to protect patients and their data.[5]

HIPAA's Security Rule requires a security management process, which is an administrative safeguard[6] that requires covered entities and business associates to "[i]mplement policies and procedures to prevent, detect, contain, and correct security violations."[7] Dating back nearly 20 years, this specification requires both a risk analysis and risk management. "Both risk analysis and risk management are standard information security processes and are critical to a covered entity's Security Rule compliance efforts."[8]

A prudent first step is identifying where protected health information (PHI) is located, as well as its ingress (pathway to the organization) and egress (pathway out of the organization). Next, utilizing the risk analysis, gaps in the requisite technical, administrative, and physical safeguards can be identified and corrected. In turn, this enables an organization, regardless of its size and location, to determine where the greatest threats are in relation to its vulnerabilities.

As attacks from insiders, outsiders, and state actors become the norm, ransomware and other types of attacks can hardly be called outliers. Yet, it is still important to appreciate "black swan" events when considering risk and the potential liabilities that arise from such events. "In 2007, statistician Nassim Nicholas Taleb defined 'Black Swan' as an event

---

5. HHS, Health Industry Cybersecurity Practices: Managing Threats and Protecting Patients (HICP 2023 edition), https://405d.hhs.gov/information (last visited Jan. 4, 2024).

6. 45 C.F.R. § 164.308(a)(1)(i).

7. *HIPAA Security Series—6 Basics of Risk Analysis and Risk Management*, Vol. 2, Paper 6, U.S. Dep't of Health & Hum. Servs. (June 2005, rev. Mar. 2007) (noting that a significant amount of the paper's content is derived from NIST and, specifically, *NIST SP 800-30—Risk Management Guide for Information Technology Systems*), https://www.hhs.gov/sites/default/files/ocr/privacy/hipaa/administrative/securityrule/riskassessment.pdf.

8. *Id.*

that 'is an outlier,' as it lies outside the realm of regular expectations. Black Swans by that definition are mostly unforeseen, rare, and can be created by geopolitical, economic, or from other unexpected events."[9] Utilizing this definition, the COVID-19 pandemic reflects a recent example.

It is undisputable that black swans raise risk management challenges, especially in the ever-evolving technological landscape.[10] For example, at the beginning of the pandemic, work shifted away from offices to the home environment where cyber safeguards were less likely to be implemented.[11] This resulted in a significant increase in cyberattacks during the first few months of the pandemic.[12] As a 2019 *Forbes* article aptly stated,

> Because of advanced computing and other emerging technologies, there are Black Swan events we can plan for, and help contain through risk management. While there are many scenarios[,] [t]here are three categories that I believe we should apply risk management principles to[,] including; 1) threats to the energy grid and critical infrastructure, 2) bio-terrorism and pandemics, and 3) the potential of malevolent artificial intelligence.[13]

Although the public sector (i.e., government) protects the nation's critical infrastructure, in the United States and other countries, it, including healthcare, is owned by private industry.[14] This underscores the notion that cyber risk management is continuous for organizations of all sizes, which leads us to the next section.

---

9. Chuck Brooks, *Risk Management and Black Swan Events,* FORBES (Oct. 23, 2019), https://www.forbes.com/sites/cognitiveworld/2019/10/23/risk-management-and-black-swan-events/?sh=308280873f61.

10. *Id.*

11. *Increasing Cybersecurity Gaps and Vulnerabilities Due to Remote Work During COVID-19,* SECURITY (June 10, 2010), https://www.securitymagazine.com/articles/92571-increasing-cybersecurity-gaps-and-vulnerabilities-due-to-remote-work-during-covid-19.

12. *INTERPOL Report Shows Alarming Rate of Cyberattacks during COVID-19,* INTERPOL (Aug. 4, 2020), https://www.interpol.int/en/News-and-Events/News/2020/INTERPOL-report-shows-alarming-rate-of-cyberattacks-during-COVID-19.

13. *Id.*

14. *Id.*

## Why Is Cyber Risk Management Relevant to an Organization's Cybersecurity Compliance?

The worldwide shift from cybersecurity to cyber risk management has led to an increase in liability for individuals within a company and on their respective boards because the net of responsibility was widened. The HHS 405(d) website highlights five cybersecurity threats and ten mitigating practices.[15] The top five threats for the healthcare sector include the following: (1) social engineering; (2) ransomware; (3) loss or theft of equipment; (4) insider, accidental, or intentional data loss; and (5) attacks against network-connected medical devices.[16]

The 405(d) Task Force also published its best practices for mitigating the risk of an attack in Technical Volumes 1 and 2. The "top 10" include the following practices:[17]

1. Email protection systems (configurations, education, and phishing)
2. Endpoint protection systems (basic endpoint protection controls)
3. Access Mmnagement (role based access, logs)
4. Data protection and loss prevention (policies, procedures, and education)
5. Asset management (inventory, procurement, and decommissioning)
6. Network management (network segmentation, physical security and guest access, and intrusion prevention)
7. Vulnerability management (identify, protect, and correct)
8. Incident response (incident response and information sharing)
9. Network-connected devices (medical device security)
10. Cybersecurity oversight and governance (policies and procedures, risk assessment and management, security awareness and training, and cyber insurance)

In sum, the suggested 405(d) Task Force practices strengthen cybersecurity capabilities in healthcare organizations and assist in mitigating risk by:

15. HHS, *supra* note 5.
16. *See* https://405d.hhs.gov/threats (last visited Jan. 4, 2024).
17. *See* Technical Volume I: Cybersecurity Practices for Small Healthcare Organizations (2023), https://405d.hhs.gov/Documents/tech-vol1-508.pdf.

- Enabling organizations to evaluate and benchmark cybersecurity capabilities effectively and reliably;
- Sharing knowledge, common practices, and appropriate references across organizations to improve cybersecurity competencies; and
- Enabling organizations to prioritize actions and investments—knowing what to ask—to improve cybersecurity.[18]

This brings us to the next section, risk utilization in the requisite risk assessment reports.

## How Is Risk Used in Risk Assessments and SSAE 18 Reports?

Effective May 1, 2017, the Statement on Standards for Attestation Engagements (SSAE) 18 "is a series of enhancements aimed to increase the usefulness and quality of SOC reports, now, superseding SSAE 16, and, obviously the relic of audit reports, SAS 70. . . . All organizations are now required to issue their System and Organization Controls (SOC) Report under SSAE-18 in a SOC 1 Report."[19] The two most significant changes to either SOC 1 or SOC 2 reports include control based changes, as well as describing the risk assessment process and the role that "subservice organizations" (in HIPAA terms, business associates and contractors, or in GDPR terms, processors) play in the overall operation of the system and corresponding controls.[20]

Subsequently, "[i]n December 2019, Statement on Standards for Attestation Engagements (SSAE) No. 19, *Agreed-Upon Procedures Engagements* was issued. SSAE 19 supersedes SSAE 18 AT-C section 215 of the same name and also amends certain provisions of SSAE 18 section 105, *Concepts Common to All Attestation Engagements*."[21] A "2020 audit of covered entities and business associates, the HHS Office of Civil Rights found that 85% of the audited entities did not meet risk assessment expectations and an even higher percentage did not meet risk

18. *Supra* note 16.
19. *See* https://ssae-16.com/ssae-16/the-ssae-18-audit-standard/ (Oct. 22, 2022).
20. *Id.*
21. *See* https://us.aicpa.org/content/dam/aicpa/research/standards/auditattest/downloadabledocuments/ssae-19-at-a-glance.pdf (last visited Jan. 4, 2024).

management expectations."[22] From a risk mitigation standpoint, utilizing the framework of SSAE 18 and/or SSAE 19 coupled with the HIPAA/NIST crosswalk and ISO 27001 provides the technical, administrative, and physical safeguards required to mitigate risk and comply with a plethora of cyber-related laws.[23]

22. Meghna Parikh, *New Considerations in Med Device Cybersecurity Compliance*, LAW360 (May 5, 2023), https://www.law360.com/health/articles/1604653?nl_pk=90f156aa-1abd-43ad-9086-7f29921666a8&utm_source=newsletter&utm_medium=email&utm_campaign=health&utm_content=2023-05-08&read_more=1&nlsidx=0&nlaidx=19?copied=1.

23. *Addressing Gaps in Cybersecurity: OCR Releases Crosswalk between HIPAA Security Rule and NIST Cybersecurity Framework*, U.S. DEP'T OF HEALTH & HUM. SERVS., https://www.hhs.gov/hipaa/for-professionals/security/nist-security-hipaa-crosswalk/index.html (last updated Feb. 23, 2016).

# CHAPTER 3

# Overview of Global Landscape of Cyberattacks, Privacy, and Security Laws

"The good we secure for ourselves is precarious and uncertain until it is secured for all of us and incorporated into our common life."

—Jane Addams

On January 26, 2023, the U.S. Department of Justice (DOJ) announced that the Federal Bureau of Information (FBI), in conjunction with the German Federal Criminal Police and Reutlingen Police Headquarters–CID Esslingen and the Netherlands National High Tech Crime Unit, infiltrated a "Hive ransomware group that has targeted more than 1,500 victims in over 80 countries around the world, including hospitals, school district[s], financial firms, and critical infrastructure."[1] This law enforcement action saved more than 1,500 victims worldwide and more than $100 million in ransom payments.[2]

With this scenario as a backdrop, the rest of the chapter delves into ransomware, contacting law enforcement, and related privacy and security laws.

## Ransomware: Malware and Types of Attacks

The easiest way to articulate the definition of ransomware is to say that it's an illegal entry and taking of information and holding it hostage until a payment is received for its return. National Institute of Standards and Technology (NIST) sets forth a more technical definition: "[r]ansomware is a type of malicious attack where attackers encrypt an

1. Press Release, U.S. Dep't of Just., U.S. Department of Justice Disrupts Hive Ransomware Variant (Jan. 26, 2023), https://www.justice.gov/opa/pr/us-department-justice-disrupts-hive-ransomware-variant.

2. *Id.*

organization's data and demand payment to restore access."[3] A common ransomware attack scenario follows:

1. A user is tricked into clicking on a malicious link that downloads a file from an external website.
2. The user executes the file, not knowing that the file is ransomware.
3. The ransomware takes advantage of vulnerabilities in the user's computer and other computers to propagate throughout the organization.
4. The ransomware simultaneously encrypts files on all the computers, then displays messages on their screens demanding payment in exchange for decrypting the files.[4]

Ransomware attacks are usually initiated via various types of phishing, which is "the fraudulent practice of sending emails or other messages purporting to be from reputable companies in order to induce individuals to reveal personal information, such as passwords and credit card numbers."[5] Or, as NIST states, "[a] technique for attempting to acquire sensitive data, such as bank account numbers, through a fraudulent solicitation in email or on a web site, in which the perpetrator masquerades as a legitimate business or reputable person."[6] Phishing, which is a form of social engineering, comes in different forms. For example:

- **Spear phishing** targets a specific group or type of individual such as a company's system administrator.
- **Whaling** targets a chief executive officer, chief financial officer, or any C-level employee within an industry or a specific business. A whaling email might state that the company is facing legal consequences and that you need to click on a link to get more information. [NOTE: whaling is often directed toward a high value target.]
- **Smishing** is an attack executed through text messaging or a short message service (SMS). A common smishing technique is

3. *Ransomware*, NIST, https://www.nist.gov/itl/smallbusinesscyber/guidance-topic/ransomware (last updated Nov. 3, 2023).

4. *Id.*

5. Oxford Languages, *phishing*.

6. NIST, *phishing*, https://csrc.nist.gov/glossary/term/phishing (last visited Jan. 6, 2024).

to deliver a message to a cell phone through SMS that contains a clickable link or a return phone number.

- **Vishing** is an attack accomplished through a voice call. A common vishing attack includes a call from someone claiming to be a representative from Microsoft. This person informs you that they have detected a virus on your computer. You are then asked to provide credit card [or banking] details so the attacker can install an updated version of anti-virus software on your computer. The attacker now has your credit card information and you have likely installed malware on your computer.[7]

What is the connection between "RaaS" and any form of phishing? First, RaaS, in the context of cyber security, is not "renin-angiotensin-aldosterone system [—] a critical regulator of blood volume and systemic vascular resistance on a long-term basis."[8] Instead, RaaS (Ransomware as a Service) is "a subscription-based model that enables affiliates to use already-developed ransomware tools to execute ransomware attacks. Affiliates earn a percentage of each successful ransom payment."[9] In essence, the affiliates, those that purchase the ransomware, deploy it through a variety of attack vectors, including phishing emails.[10] An example of a cybercriminal group that utilized RaaS is Hive.

> Hive used a ransomware-as-a-service (RaaS) model featuring administrators, sometimes called developers, and affiliates. RaaS is a subscription-based model where the developers or administrators and develop a ransomware strain and create an easy-to-use interface with which to operate it and then recruit affiliates to deploy the ransomware against victims. Affiliates identified targets and deployed this readymade malicious software to attack

7. *What Are the Different Types of Phishing?*, TRENDMICRO, https://www.trendmicro.com/en_us/what-is/phishing/types-of-phishing.html (last visited Jan. 6, 2024).

8. *Renin-Angiotensin-Aldosterone-System (RAAS)*, CLEVELAND CLINIC, https://my.clevelandclinic.org/health/articles/24175-renin-angiotensin-aldosterone-system-raas (last visited Jan. 6, 2024).

9. Edward Kost, *What Is Ransomware as a Service (RaaS)? The Dangerous Threat to World Security*, UPGUARD, https://www.upguard.com/blog/what-is-ransomware-as-a-service (last updated Nov. 15, 2023).

10. *How Does Ransomware-as-a-Service Work?*, SOPHOS, https://www.sophos.com/en-us/cybersecurity-explained/ransomware-as-a-service#:~:text=Affiliates%20sign%20up%20for%20the,phishing%20emails%20or%20exploit%20kits (last visited Jan. 6, 2024).

victim and then earned a percentage of each successful ransom payment.[11]

While various government agencies in the United States, including the Federal Bureau of Investigation (FBI) and Cybersecurity and Infrastructure Security Agency (CISA), have been issuing various advisories, thwarting attacks, and collaborating to take down various cyber threat actors,[12] the International Criminal Police Organization (INTERPOL) has been "play[ing] a key role in addressing cybercrime on a global scale in support of its 194 member countries."[13]

## What Are Law Enforcement Agencies Observing?

On December 28, 2022, *Politico* published an article related to cyberattacks and leaving patients at risk. "Cyberattacks are getting deadlier—and hospitals on the frontline are straining under increasing attacks. . . . It's time 'to view these types of attacks, ransomware attacks on hospitals, as threat-to-life crimes, not financial crimes,' said John Riggi, the national adviser for cybersecurity and risk at the American Hospital Association."[14] This scenario is not limited to the United States.

In Europe, in November 2023, data breaches and cyberattacks totaled 111,218,696. As illustrated in Table 3.1, IT Governance Europe's

11. U.S. Dep't of Just., *supra* note 1.

12. *CISA Releases Update to Royal Ransomware Advisory,* Cybersecurity & Infrastructure Security Agency (Nov. 13, 2023), https://www.cisa.gov/news-events/alerts/2023/11/13/cisa-releases-update-royal-ransomware-advisory (highlighting the inter-agency collaboration between CISA and the FBI and "provid[ing] network defenders with additional information on tactics, techniques, and procedures (TTPs) and indicators of compromise (IOCs) associated with Royal ransomware variants. FBI investigations identified these TTPs and IOCs as recently as June 2023").

13. *INTERPOL's Contribution to the Elaboration of a Comprehensive International Convention on Countering the Use of Information and Communications Technologies for Criminal Purposes,* INTERPOL (Oct. 2021), https://www.unodc.org/documents/Cybercrime/AdHocCommittee/First_session/Comments/IGOs/21COM1175-SRIUN_UseInformation_CriminalPurposes_complet.pdf.

14. Maggie Miller, *The Mounting Death Toll of Hospital Cyberattacks,* Politico (Dec. 28, 2022), https://www.politico.com/news/2022/12/28/cyberattacks-u-s-hospitals-00075638.

research uncovered a significant number of known records breached and publicly disclosed incidents.[15]

**Table 3.1** Data Breaches and Cyberattacks

| | Publicly disclosed security incidents | Records known to be breached |
|---|---|---|
| **Europe** | 139 | 111,218,696 |
| **EU** | 47 | 109,110,696 |
| **Global** | 470 | 519,111,354 |

In late 2022, André-Mignot teaching hospital, which is located in the Paris suburbs, disabled its phone and computer systems because of a ransomware attack. A significant demand was requested; however, the hospital did not intend to pay it. The hospital's services were reduced to accepting walk-ins and consultations because it was forced to partially cancel surgeries, as well as "transfer six patients from its neonatal and intensive care units to other healthcare facilities."[16] André-Mignot is not alone. Across Europe, different healthcare facilities are making headlines for either a cyberattack or a violation.[17] Like the United States, ransomware attacks in Europe are increasingly common. "According to a global study of healthcare IT professionals conducted in June 2022, 66% of healthcare organisations were hit by ransomware attacks in 2021, alarmingly up from 34% the previous year."[18] Given that the value of PHI is the highest on the black market, it is not surprising that cybercriminals are increasingly targeting medical information across a variety of data bases.[19]

15. Kyna Kosling, *Data Breaches and Cyber Attacks in Europe in November 2023—111,218,696*, IT Governance (Dec. 15, 2023), https://www.itgovernance.eu/blog/en/data-breaches-and-cyber-attacks-in-europe-in-november-2023-111218696.

16. Sergiu Gatlan, *Ransomware Attack Forces French Hospital to Transfer Patients*, Bleeping Computer (Dec. 5, 2022), https://www.bleepingcomputer.com/news/security/ransomware-attack-forces-french-hospital-to-transfer-patients/.

17. Jason O'Connor, *Ransomware Is a Growing Threat for European Healthcare Organisations*, Keeper (Apr. 21, 2023), https://www.keepersecurity.com/blog/2023/04/21/cyberattacks-soar-across-the-european-healthcare-sector/.

18. *Id.*

19. *Id.*

In Finland, a cyberattack exposed more than 40,000 patients "whose data was stolen from the Vastaamo psychotherapy center."[20]

## Contacting Law Enforcement

According to the Infosec Institute, "PHI can be worth as much as $363, [w]hile PII and credit card data only sell for around $1–$2."[21]

Cybercrime continues to generate increased interest and enforcement actions by government agencies. After an organization calls its lawyer, the next two steps should be to notify the FBI if the attack occurred on U.S. soil or if the organization is U.S. based and to notify the organization's insurance company. In the United States, the FBI promotes, "[i]f you or your organization is the victim of a network intrusion, data breach, or ransomware attack, contact your nearest FBI field office or report it at tips.fbi.gov."[22] The FBI recommends filing a report as soon as possible with the Internet Crime Complaint Center (IC3) at www.ic3.gov. The staggering number of complaints and reported losses that IC3 received between 2018 and 2022 are shown in Figure 3.1.[23]

Europe has a similar process: the European Cybercrime Centre (EC3), through Europol.[24] Although there is a central website, "[r]eporting mechanisms vary from one country to another. In Member States which do not have a dedicated online option in place, you are advised to go to your local police station to lodge a complaint."[25]

20. Melissa Heikkilä & Laurens Cerulus, *Hacker Seeks to Extort Finnish Mental Health Patients after Data Breach,* Politico (Oct. 26, 2020), https://www.politico.eu/article/cybercriminal-extorts-finnish-therapy-patients-in-shocking-attack-ransomware-blackmail-vastaamo/.

21. https://www.cisecurity.org/insights/blog/data-breaches-in-the-healthcare-sector.

22. *What You Should Know—Contact Your Local FBI Field Office,* FBI, https://www.fbi.gov/investigate/cyber#:~:text=Contact%20Your%20Local%20FBI%20Field,at%20tips.fbi.gov (last visited Jan. 6, 2024).

23. *Internet Crime Complaint Center (IC3),* FBI, https://www.ic3.gov (last visited Jan. 6, 2024).

24. *European Cybercrime Centre—EC3,* Europol, https://www.europol.europa.eu/about-europol/european-cybercrime-centre-ec3 (last updated Dec. 19, 2023).

25. *Report Cybercrime Online,* Europol, https://www.europol.europa.eu/report-a-crime/report-cybercrime-online (last updated Feb. 22, 2024).

**Figure 4.1** Complaints and Losses over the Last Five Years

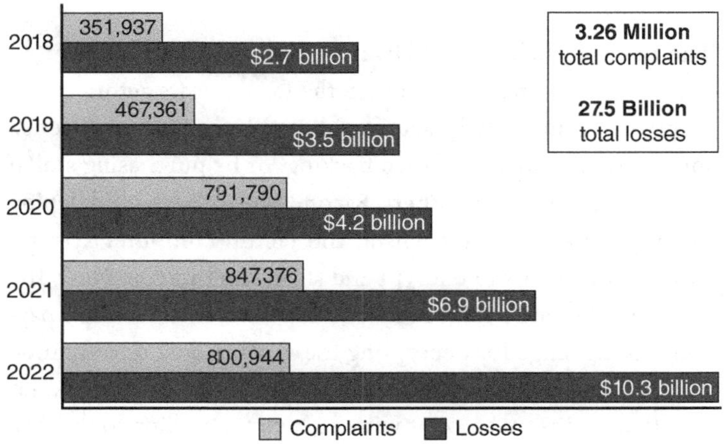


https://www.securityweek.com/fbi-cybercrime-losses-exceeded-12-5-billion-in-2023/#:~:text=Over%20the%20past%20five%20years,extortion%2C%20and%20tech%20support%20scams.

What are some "lessons learned" from Ireland that EC3 observed regarding Conti ransomware?[26] EC3 followed Conti ransomware incidents in 2021 involving "[t]argeted countries within the healthcare industry include[ing] Australia, Colombia, France, Germany, India, Italy, Netherlands, the United Kingdom, and the United States."[27] Essentially, there was a delayed deployment and subsequent shutdown of the systems in the attack that compromised the Health Service Executive of Ireland.[28] Overall, in Europe, according to the European Union Agency for Cybersecurity (ENISA) "ransomware accounts for 54% of cybersecurity threats in the health sector."[29]

26. *Lessons Learned from the HSE Cyber Attack,* HHS—Office of Information Security (Feb. 3, 2022), https://www.hhs.gov/sites/default/files/lessons-learned-hse-attack.pdf?tracking_id=060f1132ad00286e2dcb8b75b.

27. *Id.*

28. *Id.*

29. Press Release, ENISA, Checking-up on Health: Ransomware Accounts for 54% of Cybersecurity Threats (July 5, 2023), https://www.enisa.europa.eu/news/checking-up-on-health-ransomware-accounts-for-54-of-cybersecurity-threats.

In closing, with respect to Hive, which targeted more than 1,400 victims worldwide,

> The LockBit, Babuk, and Hive ransomware variants operated in the same general manner: first, the ransomware actors would identify and unlawfully access vulnerable computer systems, sometimes through their own hacking, or by purchasing stolen access credentials from others. Second, the actors would deploy the ransomware variant within the victim computer system, allowing the actors to encrypt and steal data thereon. Next, the actors would send a ransom note to the victim demanding a payment in exchange for decrypting the victim's data or refraining from sharing it publicly. Finally, the ransomware actors would negotiate a ransom amount with each victim willing to pay. If a victim did not pay, ransomware actors would often post that victim's data on a public website, often called a data leak site.
>
> Matveev is charged with conspiring to transmit ransom demands, conspiring to damage protected computers, and intentionally damaging protected computers. If convicted, he faces over 20 years in prison.[30]

In sum, contacting one's lawyer before taking any additional step is critical. Reporting to the FBI or other government law enforcement agency may be critical to mitigating liability, because the FBI, or another country's counterpart, often coordinates with other government agencies such as Health and Human Services (HHS), the Federal Trade Commission (FTC), or the Securities Exchange Commission (SEC)—agencies that have reporting requirements under a variety of laws, such as HIPAA.

30. Press Release, U.S. Dep't of Just., Russian National Charged with Ransomware Attacks against Critical Infrastructure (May 16, 2023), https://www.justice.gov/opa/pr/russian-national-charged-ransomware-attacks-against-critical-infrastructure.

## Paying (or, More Importantly, Not Paying) the Ransom Demand: Recent Guidance from the U.S. Department of the Treasury about Paying Ransomware Demands and the Potential Legal Implications

On October 1, 2020, the Office of Foreign Asset Control (OFAC) issued a Ransomware Advisory.[31] Subsequently, on September 21, 2021, it updated its guidance.[32] Here are some key take-aways:

- Paying ransom to an entity on OFAC's prohibited list, whether directly or indirectly, may result in sanctions.
- Ransomware payment may serve to prompt cybercriminals from engaging in future attacks while undermining United States' national security and policy objectives.
- "Another factor that OFAC will consider under the Enforcement Guidelines is the reporting ransomware attacks to appropriate U.S. government agencies and the nature and extent of a subject person's cooperation with OFAC, law enforcement, and other relevant agencies."[33]

Regardless of where in the world PHI resides, privacy and security laws with relevance to protected health information and the healthcare sector must be considered. Additionally, collaborating with a government's federal law enforcement agencies or local law enforcement agencies could mitigate sanctions down the line.

---

31. *Ransomware Advisory*, U.S. Dep't of Treasury—Office of Foreign Asset Control (Oct. 1, 2020), https://ofac.treasury.gov/recent-actions/20201001.

32. *Updated Advisory on Potential Sanctions Risks for Facilitating Ransomware Payments*, U.S. Dep't of Treasury—Office of Foreign Asset Control (Sept. 21, 2021), https://ofac.treasury.gov/media/912981/download?inline.

33. *Id.* at 5.

# CHAPTER 4

# Cybersecurity

## What Is Cybersecurity?

Cybersecurity, as set forth in NISTIR 8170, is "[t]he ability to protect or defend the use of cyberspace from cyber attacks."[1] *Oxford Languages* utilizes a slightly different definition: "the state of being protected against the criminal or unauthorized use of electronic data, or the measures taken to achieve this."[2] Yet, the Cybersecurity & Infrastructure Security Agency (CISA) defines it as "the art of *protecting* networks, devices, and data from unauthorized access or criminal use and *the practice of ensuring confidentiality, integrity, and availability of information.*"[3]

By way of contrast, according to NIST SP 800-29, the term "information security" is defined as "*[t]he protection of information and information systems* from unauthorized access, use, disclosure, disruption, modification, or destruction *in order to provide confidentiality, integrity, and availability.*"[4]

In comparing the various definitions of "cybersecurity" to that of "information security," the key difference appears to be that of protecting networks and infrastructure versus information. Although, it could be argued that the CISA definition encompasses both while focusing on prevention. These variations underscore the need to define the term "cybersecurity" and "information security" in policies and procedures, contracts, and training materials as it relates to cybersecurity risks and the management of those risks. "Cybersecurity risks," as defined by

---

1. *Cybersecurity*, NIST, https://csrc.nist.gov/glossary/term/cybersecurity (last visited Jan. 4, 2024).

2. Oxford Languages, *Cybersecurity*.

3. *What Is Cybersecurity?*, Cybersecurity & Infrastructure Security Agency (Feb. 1, 2021), https://www.cisa.gov/news-events/news/what-cybersecurity (emphasis added).

4. *Information Security*, NIST, https://csrc.nist.gov/glossary/term/information_security#:~:text=NIST%20SP%20800%2D209,confidentiality%2C%20integrity%2C%20and%20availability (last visited Jan. 4, 2024) (emphasis added).

the National Institute of Standards and Technology (NIST), "relate to the loss of confidentiality, integrity, or availability of information, data, or information (or control) systems and reflect the potential adverse impacts to organizational operations (i.e., mission, functions, image, or reputation) and assets, individuals, other organizations, and the Nation."[5] The remainder of this chapter provides insights into what tools are available to achieve adherence to any of these definitions of cybersecurity, which in turn can be implemented by boards, teams, and individuals to mitigate risk.

## Appreciating the Different Standards (NIST and ISO) and Their Relevance

Historically required by federal government agencies and, in turn, contractors, NIST, which falls under the umbrella of the U.S. Department of Commerce, sets the standards and publishes them in a variety of resources, which are available online.[6] NIST compliance is expressed as required in the Federal Acquisition Regulations (FAR),[7] as well as Defense Federal Acquisition Regulations (DFARS).[8]

By way of contrast, "ISO/IEC 27001 is the world's best-known standard for information security management systems (ISMS)."[9] ISO/IEC 27001 is often combined with the NIST standards set forth in publications NIST SP 800-53, rev. 5 and NIST SP 800-171 during cybersecurity audits that assess HIPAA and GDPR compliance with a variety of technical, administrative, and physical safeguards. Like NIST, ISO/IEC 27001 also applies to a variety of sectors and business sizes. When a person assesses and implements ISO/IEC 27001 standards, "this [ISMS] respects all the best practices and principles enshrined in this International Standard."[10]

---

5. *Cybersecurity Risks,* NIST, https://csrc.nist.gov/glossary/term/cybersecurity_risk#:~:text=Cybersecurity%20risks%20relate%20to%20the,individuals%2C%20other%20organizations%2C%20and%20the (last visited Jan. 4, 2024).

6. *See* https://csrc.nist.gov (last visited Jan. 4, 2024).

7. *See* https://www.ecfr.gov/current/title-48 (last updated Jan. 4, 2024).

8. *See* https://www.acquisition.gov/dfars (change effective date Jan. 4, 2024).

9. *See* https://www.iso.org/standard/27001 (last visited Jan. 4, 2024).

10. *Id.*

## Laws and General Safeguard Requirements (Technical, Administrative, and Physical)

What are technical controls (aka safeguards)? NIST defines "technical controls" as "[t]he security controls (i.e., safeguards or countermeasures) for an information system that are primarily implemented and executed by the information system through mechanisms contained in the hardware, software, or firmware components of the system."[11] Drilling down further, "security controls" are the "mechanisms contained in the hardware, software, or firmware" aspects of the information system that are implemented and executed.[12]

As set forth in NIST SP 800-12, chapter 15, there are three broad areas of physical and environmental controls:[13]

1. The physical facility is usually the building, other structure, or vehicle housing the system and network components. Systems can be characterized, based upon their operating location, as static, mobile, or portable. Static systems are installed in structures at fixed locations. Mobile systems are installed in vehicles that perform the function of a structure, but not at a fixed location. Portable systems are not installed in fixed operating locations. They may be operated in [a] wide variety of locations, including buildings or vehicles, or in the open. The physical characteristics of these structures and vehicles determine the level of such physical threats as fire, roof leaks, or unauthorized access.
2. The facility's general geographic operating location determines the characteristics of *natural threats,* which include earthquakes and flooding; *man-made threats* such as burglary, civil disorders, or interception of transmissions and emanations; and *damaging nearby activities,* including toxic chemical spills, explosions, fires, and electromagnetic interference from emitters, such as radars.
3. Supporting facilities are those services (both technical and human) that underpin the operation of the system. The system's

11. *See* NIST SP 800-137 and NIST SP 800-82, rev. 2.

12. *See* https://csrc.nist.gov/glossary/term/technical_controls (last visited Jan. 4, 2024).

13. *See* https://csrc.nist.rip/publications/nistpubs/800-12/800-12-html/chapter15.html (last visited Jan. 4, 2024).

operation usually depends on supporting facilities such as electric power, heating and air conditioning, and telecommunications. The failure or substandard performance of these facilities may interrupt operation of the system and may cause physical damage to system hardware or stored data.

The preceding guidance begs the question—given that business associates can be located internationally, in addition to the HIPAA Security Rule, what is a good framework to use? Whether or not covered entities or business associates are located in the United States or abroad, an ideal framework to use is the NIST Risk Management Framework (RMF),[14] which includes a seven-step process that an organization of any size can utilized. As a bonus, in addition to aiding persons in managing data security and privacy risks, it "links to a suite of NIST standards and guidelines to support implementation of risk management programs to meet the requirements of the Federal Information Security Modernization Act (FISMA)."[15] The seven steps are as follows:

1. **Prepare.** Identify essential activities to prepare the organization to manage security and privacy risks.
2. **Categorize.** Categorize the system and information processed, stored, and transmitted based on an impact analysis.
3. **Select.** Select the set of NIST SP 800-53 controls to protect the system based on risk assessment(s).
4. **Implement.** Implement the controls and document how controls are deployed.
5. **Assess.** Assess to determine if the controls are in place, operating as intended, and producing the desired results.
6. **Authorize.** Senior official makes a risk-based decision to authorize the system (to operate).
7. **Monitor.** Continuously monitor control implementation and risks to the system.

Utilizing the NIST RMF coupled with the HIPAA Security Rule Crosswalk to NIST Cybersecurity Framework (Crosswalk), which

---

14. *NIST Risk Management Framework Overview*, NIST, https://csrc.nist.gov/Projects/risk-management (last updated May 8, 2024).

15. *Id.*; *see also* Pub. L. No. 107-347, as amended, https://www.cisa.gov/topics/cyber-threats-and-advisories/federal-information-security-modernization-act.

is premised on the Framework for Improving Critical Infrastructure Cybersecurity,[16] which "provides a voluntary, risk-based approach—based on existing standards, guidelines, and practices—to help organizations in any industry to understand, communicate, and manage cybersecurity risks."[17] It is undisputed that persons who create, receive, maintain, and/or transmit ePHI (electronic protected health information) or EHI (electronic health information) and fall under the definitions of a covered entity or a business associate need to comply with the HIPAA Security Rule.[18]

Notably, while the Crosswalk does include all of the technical, administrative, and physical safeguard standards and implementation specifications that "map[s] to at least one of the NIST Cybersecurity Framework Subcategories, other Security Rule standards, such as specific requirements for documentation and organization, do not. *HIPAA covered entities and business associates cannot rely entirely on the crosswalk for compliance with the Security Rule.*"[19] Utilizing the various standards—NIST and ISO—to augment the HIPAA Security Rule is essential for achieving optimal compliance across jurisdictions.

## Universal Practices and Legal Requirements Related to Prevention, Detection, and Correction

A prudent place to begin is with "zero trust." According to CISA, "[z]ero trust provides a collection of concepts and ideas designed to minimize uncertainty in enforcing accurate, least privilege per-request access decisions in information systems and services in the face of a network viewed as compromised. The ultimate objective is to prevent unauthorized data access while making access control barriers as granular as possible."[20]

---

16. *See* https://www.hhs.gov/guidance/document/hipaa-security-rule-crosswalk-nist-cybersecurity-framework (last visited Jul. 13, 2024).

17. *Id.*

18. *Covered Entities and Business Associates*, U.S. Dep't of Health & Hum. Servs., https://www.hhs.gov/hipaa/for-professionals/covered-entities/index.html (last visited Jan. 4, 2024).

19. *Supra* note 16, at 1, n.3 (emphasis added).

20. *Zero Trust Maturity Model*, Cybersecurity & Infrastructure Security Agency, https://www.cisa.gov/zero-trust-maturity-model (last visited Jan. 4, 2024).

As Figure 4.1 demonstrates, there are various ways to protect identities, devices, networks, applications, and data utilizing tools ranging from visibility to automation to governance.

**Figure 4.1** High-Level Zero Trust Maturity Model Overview

https://www.cisa.gov/sites/default/files/2023-04/zero_trust_maturity_model_v2_508.pdf

Contained within the chart are a variety of technical administrative safeguards. For example encryption, tracking assets, and dynamic network configurations constitute technical safeguards. Administrative safeguards such as manual identification risk assessments, policies and procedures, training, and an annual risk analysis are all critical to cultivating a culture of compliance. As seen earlier, physical safeguards relate to "physical and environmental security controls" to protect the physical structure (i.e., building) and related access to the physical environment where the data or portions of the ISMS are housed.

As the White House announced on July 19, 2023, "[t]he new 'U.S. Cyber Trust Mark' program proposed by Federal Communications Commission (FCC) Chairwoman would raise the bar for cybersecurity across common devices including . . . smart fitness trackers, and more."[21] The cybersecurity labeling program was voted on and approved in March 2024 by the FCC and public comments are being sought before a final rule is promulgated.[22] The FCC's labeling program is founded on NIST specifications, which would include a shared responsibility model.[23] All of these initiatives are critical to ensuring privacy and security for patients, as well as covered entities and business associates, while mitigating liability through cultivating a culture of compliance.

---

21. Press Release, The White House, Biden-Harris Administration Announces Cybersecurity Labeling Program for Smart Devices to Protect American Consumers (July 18, 2023), https://www.whitehouse.gov/briefing-room/statements-releases/2023/07/18/biden-harris-administration-announces-cybersecurity-labeling-program-for-smart-devices-to-protect-american-consumers/.

22. https://docs.fcc.gov/public/attachments/DOC-401201A1.pdf (Mar. 14, 2024).

23. *Supra* note 21.

# CHAPTER 5

# HIPAA, the HITECH Act, Relevant U.S. Privacy Laws, and Some Key International Considerations

## Overview of HIPAA and the HITECH Act

The right or expectation of privacy, especially in healthcare, is not new. A 1891 U.S. Supreme Court opinion states, "[n]o right is held more sacred, or is more carefully guarded, by the common law, than the right of every individual to the possession and control of his own person."[1] Fast forward approximately 130 years and this premise remains a sine qua non of the provider–patient relationship.[2] As expressed by the American Academy of Family Physicians (AAFP):

> A confidential relationship between physician and patient is essential for the free flow of information necessary for sound medical care. Only in a setting of trust can a patient share the private feelings and personal history that enable the physician to comprehend fully, to diagnose logically, and to treat properly.[3]

In today's world, there are numerous other opportunities for patient privacy to be adversely affected, as well as for protected health information (PHI)[4] to be exfiltrated and illegally viewed and often used for

---

1. Union Pac. Ry. Co. v. Botsford, 141 U.S. 250 (May 25, 1891).

2. *Confidentiality, Patient/Physician*, Am. Academy of Family Physicians, https://www.aafp.org/about/policies/all/confidentiality-patient-physician.html#:~:text=Historically%2C%20the%20privileged%20nature%20of,legislative%20action%20and%20case%20law (last visited July 13, 2023).

3. *Id.*

4. 45 C.F.R. § 160.103. PHI means information in any form or medium that is received by Business Associate from or on behalf of Covered Entity, is created by Business Associate, or is made accessible to Business Associate by Covered Entity regarding the past,

personal financial gain.[5] These considerations also raise additional legal, bioethical, and reputational issues. Hence, the purpose of this chapter is to explain patient privacy and provider duties under the Health Insurance Portability and Accountability Act of 1996 (HIPAA), involving the 21st Century Cures Act, and Federal Trade Commission data privacy and security enforcement actions. States have also been joining the "craze," with numerous states passing data privacy and security laws to give consumers further protections.

## *HIPAA's Privacy Rule*

Subsequent to HIPAA being signed into law on August 21, 1996, a series of rules were promulgated by the U.S. Department of Health and Human Services (HHS), the first of which was the Privacy Rule.[6] There are three categories of persons who must comply with HIPAA, as well as comply with the Privacy Rule, Security Rule, and Breach Notification Rule.[7] The three categories are covered entity, business associate, and subcontractor.[8] A covered entity means the following: (1) health plan, (2) healthcare clearing house, and (3) healthcare provider who transmits any health information in electronic form in connection with a transaction covered by this subchapter.[9] A business associate essentially is a person who creates,

present or future physical/mental condition of an individual, the provision of healthcare to an individual, or the past, present or future payment for the provision of healthcare to an individual, and that identifies the individual or with respect to which there is a reasonable basis to believe the information can be used to identify the individual. For purposes of this article, PHI is used generally to also include electronic protected health information (ePHI) (also defined in 45 C.F.R. § 160.103), and electronic health information (EHI) as defined in 45 C.F.R. § 171.102.

5. Press Release, U.S. Dep't of Just., Former Hospital Employee Indicted for Criminal HIPAA Violations (July 3, 2014), https://www.justice.gov/usao-edtx/pr/former-hospital-employee-indicted-criminal-hipaa-violations; *see also Ransomware Activity Targeting Healthcare and Public Health Sector*, CYBERSECURITY & INFRASTRUCTURE SECURITY AGENCY, https://www.cisa.gov/uscert/ncas/alerts/aa20-302a (last revised Nov. 2, 2020).

6. CENTERS FOR MEDICARE AND MEDICAID SERVICES, HIPAA BASICS FOR PROVIDERS: PRIVACY, SECURITY, & BREACH NOTIFICATION RULES, https://www.cms.gov/Outreach-and-Education/Medicare-Learning-Network-MLN/MLNProducts/Downloads/HIPAAPrivacyandSecurity.pdf (last visited Jan. 15, 2023).

7. *Id.*

8. 45 C.F.R. § 160.103, https://www.ecfr.gov/current/title-45/subtitle-A/subchapter-C/part-160 (last visited July 15, 2023).

9. *Id.*

receives, maintains, or transmits PHI on behalf of a covered entity for a purpose set forth in the definition.[10] A subcontractor "creates, receives, maintains, or transmits [PHI] on behalf of the business associate."[11]

These are the three categories under HIPAA, which is a federal law. Some states, like Texas,[12] have a broader definition of "covered entity," which includes the federal definitions of covered entity, business associate, and subcontractor. Hence, the application of various requirements in certain states extends beyond the three HIPAA categories.

The May 12, 2021, executive order[13] reinforces what the past four administrations have espoused—the United States is vulnerable to cyberattacks, and it will take a collaborative effort between the public and private sectors to ensure that the U.S. government and private persons are protected. This executive order goes a step further to highlight the importance of prevention, detection, and correction in order to remediate the risks of cybersecurity incidents. "A major goal of the Privacy Rule is to assure that individuals' health information is properly protected while allowing the flow of health information needed to provide and promote high quality health care and to protect the public's health and well being."[14] The Privacy Rule has a variety of obligations for covered entities and business associates. For example:

- Covered entities are required to provide a notice of privacy practices, which is a writing that is basic in nature and sets forth the individual's rights related to his/her PHI and the privacy practices of healthcare providers and health plans.[15]

10. *Id.*

11. *Id.*

12. Tex. Health & Safety Code § 181 (defining "the term 'covered entity' [to] include a business associate, health care payer, governmental unit, information or computer management entity, school, health researcher, health care facility, clinic, health care provider, or person who maintains an Internet site").

13. Press Release, The White House, Executive Order on Improving the Nation's Cybersecurity (May 12, 2021), https://www.whitehouse.gov/briefing-room/presidential-actions/2021/05/12/executive-order-on-improving-the-nations-cybersecurity/.

14. *Summary of the HIPAA Privacy Rule*, U.S. Dep't of Health & Hum. Servs., https://www.hhs.gov/hipaa/for-professionals/privacy/laws-regulations/index.html (last visited Jan. 21, 2023).

15. *Model Notices of Privacy Practices*, U.S. Dep't of Health & Hum. Servs., https://www.hhs.gov/hipaa/for-professionals/privacy/guidance/model-notices-privacy-practices/index.html (last visited Jan. 21, 2023).

- Unless an exception exists, such as disclosing diseases to a governmental public health entity, covered entities need to obtain authorization to disclose patient information. The best way to do this is by having the patient or the patient's legally authorized representative fill out a written HIPAA authorization form.[16]
- Right of access requires that patients be provided with a copy of their designated health record set[17] and verify that the person requesting the information is authorized to do so.[18] "For those covered entities providing individuals with access to their PHI through web portals, those portals should already be set up with appropriate authentication controls, as required by 45 CFR 164.312(d) of the HIPAA Security Rule, to ensure that the person seeking access is the individual or the individual's personal representative."[19]
- Notably, there are two categories of information that the right of access does not cover—psychotherapy notes[20] and information compiled in reasonable anticipation of a legal proceeding, whether civil, criminal, or administrative.[21] "The underlying PHI from the individual's medical or payment records or other records used to generate the above types of excluded records or information remains part of the designated record set and subject to access by the individual."[22]

These privacy considerations are important because of the trust that is inherent in the patient–physician relationship. One area of interest to HHS-OCR, which relates to the patient–provider relationship is the obligation to provide patients with timely access to their medical records, that is, within 30 days.[23] One important note: states often require that

---

16. 45 C.F.R. § 164.524(b)(1).
17. *Id.* § 164.501.
18. *Id.* § 164.514(h).
19. *Summary of the HIPAA Privacy Rule, supra* note 14.
20. 45 C.F.R. §§ 164.524(a)(1)(i), 164.501.
21. *Id.* § 164.524(a)(1)(ii).
22. *Summary of the HIPAA Privacy Rule, supra* note 14.
23. David Raths, *OCR Announces 11 Enforcement Actions in Right of Access Initiative,* Healthcare Innovation (July 21, 2022), https://www.hcinnovationgroup.com/cybersecurity/hipaa/news/21274953/ocr-announces-11-enforcement-actions-in-right-of-access-initiative.

medical records are provided in fewer than 30 days. In Texas, for example, the Texas Administrative Code section 165.2(b) expressly references HIPAA and requires covered entities to provide medical and billing records within 15 days.[24] For this, and the reasons set forth as follows, covered entities and business associates should be vigilant about having processes in place for providing medical and financial records to patients in the requisite timeframe while protecting patient privacy and their own cybersecurity.

HR 7898 was signed into law on January 5, 2021. It defines "recognized security practices" and amends the HITECH Act.[25] HR 7898 should be incorporated into the annual risk analysis and policies and procedures because it essentially creates a safe harbor, so long as the covered entity or business associate has adequately demonstrated that it had, for not less than the previous 12 months, recognized security practices in place that may—

1. mitigate fines under section 1176 of the Social Security Act (as amended by section 13410);
2. result in the early, favorable termination of an audit under section 13411; and
3. mitigate the remedies that would otherwise be agreed to in any agreement with respect to resolving potential violations of the HIPAA Security rule (part 160 of title 45 Code of Federal Regulations and subparts A and C of part 164 of such title) between the covered entity or business associate and the Department of Health and Human Services.[26]

The 21st Century Cures Act builds upon the Privacy Rule.

---

24. *See* https://texreg.sos.state.tx.us/public/readtac$ext.TacPage?sl=R&app=9&p_dir=&p_rloc=&p_tloc=&p_ploc=&pg=1&p_tac=&ti=22&pt=9&ch=165&rl=2 (last visited Jan. 21, 2023).

25. Health Information Technology for Economic and Clinical Health Act, Pub. L. No. 116-321 (Jan. 5, 2021), https://www.congress.gov/bill/116th-congress/house-bill/7898/text.

26. Rachel V. Rose, *Cybersecurity: Look to Where You Are Going*, Physicians Practice (Feb. 11, 2021), https://www.physicianspractice.com/view/cybersecurity-look-to-where-you-are-going (emphasis added).

## 21st Century Cures Act

The 21st Century Cures Act of 2016 (Cures Act) addresses interoperability, information blocking, and Office of the National Coordinator (ONC) for Health IT Certification; expands the right of patients to access their electronic health information (EHI); and requires that providers give patients access to their EHI in the form of their choosing.[27] Cures Act section 4004 addresses "information blocking," which is germane to maintaining a secure IT environment and providing patients with access to their medical records. The Cures Act, as well as the two final rules (ONC Final Rule and CMS Final Rule[28])[29] implementing the Cures Act are dense and have provisions that are not obvious upon the first read.

"Information blocking is a practice by a health IT developer of certified health IG, health information network, health information exchange, or health care provider that, except as required by law or specified by HHS as a reasonable and necessary activity, is likely to interfere with access, exchange, or use of electronic health information (EHI)." As set forth in 45 C.F.R. § 171.102:

> EHI means electronic protected health information [ePHI] as defined in 45 CFR 160.103 to the extent that it would be included in a designated record set as defined in 45 CFR 164.501, regardless of whether the group of records are used or maintained by or for a covered entity as defined in 45 CFR 164.103, but EHI shall not include: (1) Psychotherapy notes as defined in 45 CFR 164.501; or (2) Information compiled in reasonable anticipation of, or for use in, a civil, criminal, or administrative action or proceeding.[30]

27. Pub. L. No. 114-255 (Dec. 13, 2016). ONC Health IT Certification was initially launched in 2010 as part of the program formerly known as the Medicare and Medicaid EHR Incentive Program and renamed the Promoting Interoperability Programs.

28. Information blocking is generally mentioned less than ten times in the CMS Final Rule. Therefore, the CMS Final Rule is not a focus of this publication.

29. Rachel V. Rose, *Two Final Rules Related to 21st Century Cures Act Released during Pandemic*, Physicians Practice (Apr. 23, 2020), https://www.physicianspractice.com/view/two-final-rules-related-21st-century-cures-act-released-during-pandemic.

30. 45 C.F.R. § 171.102, https://www.law.cornell.edu/cfr/text/45/171.102 (last visited Jan. 21, 2023).

Covered entities, including neurologists, have an obligation under HIPAA and the 21st Century Cures Act to provide certain EHI to patients without interference. Otherwise, it may be considered information blocking.[31] While section 4004 of the Cures Act establishes the general prohibition against the following forms of information blocking, it also provides eight exceptions.[32] The following practices likely constitute information blocking:

- Practices that restrict authorized access, exchange, or use, under applicable state or federal law, of such information for treatment and other permitted purposes under such applicable law, including transitions between certified health information technologies (health IT).
- Implementing health IT in nonstandard ways that are likely to substantially increase the complexity or burden of accessing, exchanging, or using EHI.
- Implementing health IT in ways that are likely to (1) restrict the access, exchange, or use of EHI with respect to exporting complete information sets or in transitioning between health IT systems; or (2) lead to fraud, waste, or abuse, or impede innovations and advancements in health information access, exchange, and use, including care delivery enabled by health IT.

Section 4004 of the Cures Act's exceptions creates a balance between cybersecurity considerations, a covered entity or business associate's obligations to other patients and its overall IT security, and an individual's right to access his/her medical records in a format of his/her choosing.[33]

---

31. *Id.* § 171.103, https://www.law.cornell.edu/cfr/text/45/171.103 (last visited Jan. 21, 2021).

32. *Supra* note 8.

33. ONC, *ONC's Cures Act Final Rule Supports Seamless and Secure Access, Exchange, and Use of Electronic Health Information*, https://www.healthit.gov/curesrule/ (last visited May 31, 2024). As a related matter, it is important to remember that Certified API Developers and API Information Sources (i.e., healthcare organizations) are required to adopt standardized application programming interfaces (APIs) in order to assist patients in accessing EHI through smartphone applications in a secure and easily accessible manner. *See* ONC, *Cures Act Final Rule—Application Programming Interfaces (APIs) Conditions and Maintenance of Certification* https://www.healthit.gov/sites/default/files/page2/2020-03/APIConditionsandMaintenance.pdf (last visited Jan. 19, 2023) (emphasizing Section

Table 5.1 sets forth the exceptions to information blocking.[34] There are two categories of exceptions related to providing patients with EHI: (1) not fulfilling requests and (2) exceptions involving the procedures for fulfilling requests.

**Table 5.1**

| Category of the Exception | Exception |
|---|---|
| Not fulfilling requests to access, exchange, or use EHI | **Preventing Harm Exception** applies when an actor engages in practices that are reasonable and necessary to prevent harm to a patient or another person, provided certain conditions are met. |
| Not fulfilling requests to access, exchange, or use[35] EHI | **Privacy Exception** applies if an actor does not fulfill a request to access, exchange, or use EHI to protect an individual's privacy, provided certain conditions are met.[36] |
| Not fulfilling requests to access, exchange, or use EHI | **Security Exception** applies if an actor interferes with the access, exchange, or use of EHI to protect the security of EHI, provided certain conditions are met. NOTE: the actions must be directly related to safeguarding the confidentiality, integrity, and availability of EHI that is tailored to specific security risks and implemented in a uniform and nondiscriminatory manner. |
| Not fulfilling requests to access, exchange, or use EHI | **Infeasibility Exception** applies if an actor does not fulfill a request to access, exchange, or use EHI due to the infeasibility of the request, provided certain conditions are met. |
| Not fulfilling requests to access, exchange, or use EHI | **Health IT Performance Exception** applies when an actor takes reasonable and necessary measures to make health IT temporarily unavailable or to degrade the health IT's performance for the benefit of the overall performance of the health IT, provided certain conditions are met. |

4002 of the Cures Act and the requirements of Certification for health IT developers participating in the ONC Health IT Certification Program).

34. *Cures Act Final Rule Information Blocking Exceptions*, ONC, https://www.healthit.gov/cures/sites/default/files/cures/2020-03/InformationBlockingExceptions.pdf (last visited Jan. 13, 2023).

35. *Id.*

36. The HIPAA Privacy Rule, 45 C.F.R. § 164.525(a)(1), (2), applies.

| Category of the Exception | Exception |
|---|---|
| Exceptions that involve procedures for fulfilling requests to access, exchange, or use EHI | **Content and Manner Exception** is available to an actor to limit the content of its response to a request to access, exchange, or use EHI or the way it fulfills a request to access, exchange, or use EHI, provided certain conditions are met. |
| Exceptions that involve procedures for fulfilling requests to access, exchange, or use EHI | **Fees Exception** enables an actor to charge fees, including fees that result in a reasonable profit margin, for accessing, exchanging, or using EHI, provided certain conditions are met. NOTE: must comply with section 170.402(a)(4) or section 170.404. |
| Exceptions that involve procedures for fulfilling requests to access, exchange, or use EHI | **Licensing Exception** allows for an actor to license interoperability elements for EHI to be accessed, exchanged, or used, provided certain conditions are met. |

These eight exceptions (i.e., healthcare providers, health IT developers, health information networks (HINs), and health information exchanges (HIEs)) will enable the conduct not to be information blocking if all the requirements for the individual exception are met.

On July 3, 2023, the HHS—Office of the Inspector General (OIG) published "Grants, Contracts, and Other Agreements: Fraud and Abuse; Information Blocking; Office of Inspector General's Civil Money Penalty Rules" in the *Federal Register*.[37] The final rule implements three statutory provisions related to different laws: (1) 21st Century Cures Act's amendment of the Public Health Service Act (PHSA),[38] which enables OIG to investigate information blocking claims and authorizes HHS to investigate information blocking claims; (2) amend the Civil Monetary Penalties Law (CMPL) to impose CMPs, assessments, and exclusions upon persons that engage in fraud and other misconduct related to HHS grants, and so on;[39] and (3) increase the penalty amounts in the CMPL related to the BiPartisan Budget Act of 2018 (BBA 2018).[40]

37. 88 Fed. Reg. 42820 (July 3, 2023) (noting that most of the items became effective on Aug. 2, 2023, with the exception of §§ 1003.1400, 1410, and 1420 (instruction 10), which are effective Sept. 1, 2023), https://www.federalregister.gov/documents/2023/07/03/2023-13851/grants-contracts-and-other-agreements-fraud-and-abuse-information-blocking-office-of-inspector.

38. 42 U.S.C. § 300jj-52.

39. Id. § 1320a–7a.

40. Pub. L. No. 115–123.

Consider a practical example: a patient requests his/her EHI from a physician's electronic health record system to be sent to their Tik-Tok or other social media account. First, the physician's office, as a covered entity, has an obligation to provide the patient with the requested records within 30 days unless notice is given and a valid reason exists for an additional 30-day extension.[41] Second, as a general rule, patients have the right to request that their EHI be sent to the location of their choosing. Third, just because a location like Tik-Tok or an unknown app is the requested receiving point does not mean that the physician's office or its business associate must comply. Finally, the appropriate Cures Act exception must be identified, and written notice must be provided to the patient stating that the requested delivery location is not possible, state the exception that applies, and provide an alternative method/location (e.g., secure email). This balances the covered entity's obligation to provide the EHI to the patient within 30 days with its parallel obligation to protect a patient's privacy and the overall cybersecurity of its IT infrastructure and electronic health records.

## Select U.S. Privacy Laws

While most people are most familiar with the California Consumer Protection Act (CCPA), which was the first comprehensive consumer privacy law, and its successor the California Privacy Rights Act (CPRA), they may not be as familiar with the other states that have followed suit.[42] An easy way to think about CCPA/CPRA is to analogize it to General Data Protection Regulation (GDPR)—remembering that CCPA/CPRA protects California residents and GDPR protects any individual residing within or located in the EU. Although there are many similarities, a key distinguishing factor is that CCPA/CPRA requires individuals to opt out, whereas GDPR requires individuals to opt in.[43]

---

41. 45 C.F.R. § 164.524; *see also* https://www.hhs.gov/hipaa/for-professionals/privacy/guidance/access/index.html (last visited Jan. 21, 2023).

42. *See CPRA vs CCPA: What You Need to Know About the Replacement of CCPA in 2023*, Secuvy (Dec. 9, 2022), https://secuvy.ai/blog/cpra-vs-ccpa-what-you-need-to-know-about-the-replacement-of-ccpa-in-2023/#:~:text=CPRA%20vs%20CCPA%3A%20What%20You,need%20to%20be%20aware%20of.

43. Comparing Privacy Laws: GDPR v. CCPA (Nov. 2018), https://fpf.org/wp-content/uploads/2018/11/GDPR_CCPA_Comparison-Guide.pdf.

In addition to California, as of June 30, 2023, Iowa, Indiana, Florida, Montana, Texas, Tennessee, and Oregon have all passed comprehensive data privacy laws. Virginia, Colorado, and Washington, among most other states, also have state privacy laws.[44] Two key items from the Oregon Consumer Privacy Act (OCPA) are as follows:

> Unlike some state privacy laws, the OCPA lacks some of the relatively common entity-level exemptions. For example, the OCPA does not exempt covered entities within the meaning of the Health Insurance Portability and Accountability Act or entities covered by the Gramm-Leach-Bliley Act. However, it does permit numerous data-level exemptions for data covered by federal law.
>
> Like Colorado's law, the OCPA does not generally exempt non-profits. However, there is a limited non-profit exemption for organizations that (1) are established to detect and prevent fraudulent acts associated with insurance, or (2) provide programming to radio or television networks. Moreover, the OCPA has a one-year exemption for all non-profits until July 1, 2025.[45]

The key take-away is that each law is nuanced, with its own definitions, exclusions, and requirements. It is imperative to appreciate what portions overlap and what portions need to be parsed out and addressed to ensure compliance.

## The Federal Trade Commission and the Securities and Exchange Commission

Typically, people associate privacy and security violations involving Individually Identifiable Health Information (IIHI) with HIPAA and HHS-OCR. Although its Health Breach Notification Rule (HBNR) has been around since 2009 (16 C.F.R. part 318) and there have been other enforcement actions not utilizing the FTC's HBNR but utilizing the Federal Trade Commission Act to protect consumers from privacy and

44. *Oregon to Become Next State to Enact Comprehensive Data Privacy Law,* Am. Health Law Ass'n, (June 30, 2023), https://www.lexology.com/library/detail.aspx?g=4faf1f99-2f00-48be-adeb-cf7e568f1827.

45. *Id.*

security issues perpetrated by different companies (i.e., CVS (February 18, 2009) and Henry Schein (May 23, 2016)), the first enforcement action involving the HBNR did not occur until February 1, 2023.[46]

While it has some language similarities to the HBNR, it is not limited to covered entities, business associates, and subcontractors, as defined in 45 C.F.R. § 160.103. Also, the Federal Trade Commission's (FTC's) enforcement authority is derived from section 5—The Federal Trade Commission Act of 1914 as amended. Two recent enforcement action settlements, which occurred between February and early March 2023, underscore its authority, and both are notable for distinct reasons:[47]

- GoodRx (**February 1, 2023**). GoodRx is the first case where an enforcement action was taken under the FTC's Health Breach Notification Rule. Here, GoodRx, a telehealth and prescription drug discount provider "fail[ed] to notify consumers and other of its unauthorized disclosures of consumers' personal health information to Facebook, Google, and other companies." Moreover, "[i]n a first-of-its-kind proposed order, filed by the Department of Justice on behalf of the FTC, GoodRx will be prohibited from sharing user health data with applicable third parties for advertising purposes, and has agreed to pay a $1.5 million civil penalty for violating the rule. The proposed order must be approved by the federal court to go into effect." GoodRx paid the government $7.8 million to settle the allegations.[48]
- BetterHelp, Inc. (**March 2, 2023**). In another first-of-its-kind case, the FTC provided remuneration to customers who were harmed by "online counseling service BetterHelp [, which] revealed consumers' sensitive data with third parties such as Facebook and Snapchat for advertising after promising to keep such data private."[49]

46. Rachel V. Rose, *The New Kid on the Block: The Federal Trade Commission and Data Sharing*, Physicians Practice (Mar. 9, 2023), https://www.physicianspractice.com/view/the-new-kid-on-the-block-the-federal-trade-commission-and-data-sharing.

47. *Id.*

48. *See* https://www.ftc.gov/news-events/news/press-releases/2023/02/ftc-enforcement-action-bar-goodrx-sharing-consumers-sensitive-health-info-advertising (Feb. 1, 2023).

49. *See* https://www.ftc.gov/legal-library/browse/cases-proceedings/2023169-betterhelp-inc-matter (Mar. 2, 2023).

In addition to the FTC, the U.S. Securities Exchange Commission (SEC) is another government agency that has enforcement authority related to securities laws' violations. While testifying in front of the U.S. Senate Committee on Banking, Housing, and Urban Affairs, SEC Chairman Gary Gensler stated, "[t]he proposed amendments are intended to better inform investors about a registrant's risk management, strategy, and governance and to provide timely notification of material cybersecurity incidents."[50] The waiting is over. On July 26, 2023, the SEC announced that it released the final rule related to cybersecurity. Specifically, it requires registrants and foreign issuers alike "to disclose material cybersecurity incidents they experience and to disclose on an annual basis material information regarding their cybersecurity risk management, strategy, and governance."[51]

When reading the final rules, one should consider doing so with an eye toward risk, governance, materiality, and legal implications. Page 117 captures the essence of what standards (i.e., National Institute of Standards and Technologies (NIST))[52] and laws should also be considered:[53]

> Some registrants are also subject to other mandates regarding cybersecurity risk management, strategy, and governance. For instance, government contractors may be subject to the Federal Information Security Modernization Act, and use the NIST framework to manage information and privacy risks. Certain financial institutions may be subject to the FTC's Standards for Safeguarding Customer Information Rule, requiring an information security program, including a qualified individual to oversee the security program, and the provision of periodic reports on the cybersecurity program to a company's board of directors or equivalent governing body. Under HIPAA regulations, covered

---

50. 87 Fed. Reg. 16590. See also Gary Gensler, Testimony before the United States Senate Committee on Banking, Housing, and Urban Affairs (Sept. 15, 2022), https://www.sec.gov/news/testimony/gensler-testimony-housing-urban-affairs-091522.

51. Press Release, SEC, SEC Adopts Rules on Cybersecurity Risk Management, Strategy, Governance, and Incident Disclosure by Public Companies (July 26, 2023), https://www.sec.gov/news/press-release/2023-139.

52. NIST, https://www.nist.gov/about-nist (last visited Aug. 1, 2023).

53. SEC, *Final Rules (Not Yet Published in the Federal Register)*, at 117 (July 26, 2023), https://www.sec.gov/corpfin/secg-cybersecurity#:~:text=On%20July%2026%2C%202023%2C%20the,Exchange%20Act%20of%201934%20(the internal citations omitted).

> entities are subject to rules that require protection against reasonably anticipated threats to electronic protected health information. International jurisdictions also have cybersecurity risk mitigation measures and governance requirements (see, for example, the GDPR). These rules and regulations provide varying standards and requirements for disclosing cybersecurity risk management, strategy, and governance, and may not provide investors with public or clear and comparable disclosure regarding how a particular registrant manages its cybersecurity risk profile.

As a reminder, despite the SEC final rules only mentioning HIPAA-covered entities, business associates, which include subcontractors,[54] are also required to meet these standards.[55] Additionally,

> [i]f a covered entity engages a business associate to help it carry out its health care activities and functions, the covered entity must have a written business associated contract or other arrangement [written agreement] with the business associate that establishes specifically what the business associate has been engaged to do and requires the business associate to comply with the Rules' requirements to protect the privacy and security of protected health information. *In addition to these contractual obligations, business associates are directly liable for compliance with certain provisions of the HIPAA Rules.*[56]

These "contractual obligations" are set forth in a business associate agreement (BAA)[57] or other similar agreement.[58] Hence, the underlying compliance with HIPAA and other laws, such as GDPR, especially if a business associate is located outside of the United States,[59] is not optional

---

54. 45 C.F.R. § 160.103.

55. *Covered Entities and Business Associates*, U.S. Dep't of Health & Hum. Servs., https://www.hhs.gov/hipaa/for-professionals/covered-entities/index.html (last visited Aug. 1, 2023).

56. *Id.* (emphasis added).

57. 45 C.F.R. § 164.504.

58. *See What Is a GDPR Data Processing Agreement?*, DGPR.EU, https://gdpr.eu/what-is-data-processing-agreement/ (last visited Aug. 1, 2023).

59. Rachel V. Rose, *HIPAA Considerations When Business Associates and Data Are International*, NAMAS (Dec. 9, 2022), https://namas.co/hipaa-considerations-when-business-associates-and-data-are-international/.

and can translate into liability under a variety of SEC laws, rules, and regulations, including its recent final rule.[60]

Overall, there are multiple fronts that persons, both in the United States and outside the United States, need to consider when assessing risk and complying with the variety of privacy and security laws.

60. Press Release, SEC, SEC Announces Three Actions Charging Deficient Cybersecurity Procedures (Aug. 30, 2021), https://www.sec.gov/news/press-release/2021-169.

# CHAPTER 6

# GDPR and Member State Laws

"At the end of the day, the goals are simple: safety and security."

—Jodi Rell

Touted as the most rigorous privacy and security data protection law in the world, the General Data Protection Regulation (GDPR) came into effect on May 25, 2018. It is notable for many reasons, including its harsh fines, the ability of individual member states to adopt the European Union (EU) law outright or add criminal violations and other items, and giving European citizens control over their data in most instances, as well as protecting them from persons who attempt to target and/or collect their data without their knowledge and consent.[1] Importantly, under GDPR, "health data is considered a special category of data, so more rigorous protections exist for it than with other types of personal data."[2] This chapter focuses on key aspects of GDPR, as well as on how U.S. persons can use the DRAFT NIST Cybersecurity Framework 2.0 (CSF 2.0) and take an offensive instead of a defensive approach, including remote work settings.

## Overview of GDPR and Its Application to Member States

The EU's GDPR was designed to apply to all types of businesses, from large multinational corporations to small persons. Article 1 addresses the general subject-matter and objectives, which includes three items:

1. This Regulation lays down rules relating to the protection of natural persons with regard to the processing of personal data and rules relating to the free movement of personal data.

---

1. *What Is GDPR, the EU's New Data Protection Law?*, EU, https://gdpr.eu/what-is-gdpr/ (last visited Aug. 23, 2023).

2. *The Relationship between GDPR and Healthcare Data*, FORTRA, https://www.goanywhere.com/blog/gdpr-and-its-relationship-with-healthcare#:~:text=The%20Relationship%20Between%20GDPR%20and,collected%20and%20where%20it%27s%20stored (last visited Aug. 23, 2023).

2. This Regulation protects fundamental rights and freedoms of natural persons and in particular their right to protection of personal data.
3. The free movement of personal data within the Union shall be neither restricted nor prohibited for reasons connected with the protection of natural persons with regard to the processing of personal data.

Building on Article 1, two of the most important definitions in GDPR are "controller" and "processor," which are found in Chapter 1 (Article 4) and expanded upon in Chapter 4 (Articles 24–43).[3] Chapter 1, Article 4 (7), (8), sets forth the following explanations:

> (7) "controller" means the natural or legal person, public authority, agency or other body which, alone or jointly with others, determines the purposes and means of the processing of personal data; where the purposes and means of such processing are determined by Union or Member State law, the controller or the specific criteria for its nomination may be provided for by Union or Member State law;
>
> (8) "processor" means a natural or legal person, public authority, agency or other body which processes personal data on behalf of the controller[.]
>
> Appreciating these terms is important, as well as that of a third party who acts as a subprocessor. There is also a contract under GDPR between a controller and a processor or a processor and a subprocessor—Data Processing Agreement—that is like a HIPAA business associate agreement (BAA). An example of one follows:[4]

**SAMPLE DATA PROCESSING AGREEMENT**

This Data Processing Agreement ("**Agreement**") forms part of the Contract for Services ("**Principal Agreement**") between ___________ ______________ (the "Company") and __________________(the "**Data Processor**"). Collectively, these persons are known as the "**Parties.**"

---

3. *See* https://gdpr-info.eu/art-4-gdpr/ (last visited Aug. 31, 2023).

4. *Data Processing Agreement (Template)*, EU, https://gdpr.eu/data-processing-agreement/ (last visited Aug. 31, 2023) (noting that the opening paragraph was altered by the book authors and a "WHEREAS" statement was added).

**WHEREAS, the** Company acts as a Data Controller;

**WHEREAS,** the Company wishes to subcontract certain Services, which imply the processing of personal data, to the Data Processor;

**WHEREAS,** Parties seek to implement a data processing agreement that complies with the requirements of the current legal framework in relation to data processing and with the Regulation (EU) 2016/679 of the European Parliament and of the Council of 27 April 2016 on the protection of natural persons with regard to the processing of personal data and on the free movement of such data, and repealing Directive 95/46/EC (General Data Protection Regulation);

**WHEREAS,** Parties attest that they have adequate technical, administrative, and physical safeguards in place; and

**WHEREAS,** Parties wish to lay down their rights and obligations.

**NOW, WHEREFORE,** IT IS AGREED AS FOLLOWS:

1. Definitions and Interpretation.
   - 1.1 Unless otherwise defined herein, capitalized terms and expressions used in this Agreement shall have the following meaning:
     - 1.1.1 "**Agreement**" means this Data Processing Agreement and all Schedules.
     - 1.1.2 "**Company Personal Data**" means any Personal Data Processed by a Contracted Processor on behalf of Company pursuant to or in connection with the Principal Agreement.
     - 1.1.3 "**Contracted Processor**" means a Subprocessor.
     - 1.1.4 "**Data Protection Laws**" means EU Data Protection Laws and, to the extent applicable, the data protection or privacy laws of any other country.
     - 1.1.5 "**EEA**" means the European Economic Area.
     - 1.1.6 "**EU Data Protection Laws**" means EU Directive 95/46/EC, as transposed into domestic legislation of each Member State and as amended, replaced or superseded from time to time, including by the GDPR and laws implementing or supplementing the GDPR.

1.1.7 "**GDPR**" means EU General Data Protection Regulation 2016/679.

1.1.8 "**Data Transfer**" means:

1.1.8.1 a transfer of Company Personal Data from the Company to a Contracted Processor; or

1.1.8.2 an onward transfer of Company Personal Data from a Contracted Processor to a Subcontracted Processor, or between two establishments of a Contracted Processor, in each case, where such transfer would be prohibited by Data Protection Laws (or by the terms of data transfer agreements put in place to address the data transfer restrictions of Data Protection Laws).

1.1.9 "**Services**" means the ______________________ services the Company provides.

1.1.10 "**Subprocessor**" means any person appointed by or on behalf of Processor to process Personal Data on behalf of the Company in connection with the Agreement.

1.2 The terms, "Commission," "Controller," "Data Subject," "Member State," "Personal Data," "Personal Data Breach," "Processing" and "Supervisory Authority" shall have the same meaning as in the GDPR, and their cognate terms shall be construed accordingly.

2. Processing of Company Personal Data.

2.1 Processor shall:

2.1.1 comply with all applicable Data Protection Laws in the Processing of Company Personal Data; and

2.1.2 not Process Company Personal Data other than on the relevant Company's documented instructions.

2.2 The Company instructs Processor to process Company Personal Data.

3. Processor Personnel.

Processor shall take reasonable steps to ensure the reliability of any employee, agent or contractor of any Contracted Processor who may have access to the Company Personal Data, ensuring in each case that access is strictly limited to those individuals who need to know / access the relevant Company Personal Data, as strictly necessary for the purposes of the Principal Agreement, and to comply with Applicable Laws in the context of that individual's duties to the Contracted Processor, ensuring that all such individuals are subject to confidentiality undertakings or professional or statutory obligations of confidentiality.

4. Security.
   4.1 Taking into account the state of the art, the costs of implementation and the nature, scope, context and purposes of Processing as well as the risk of varying likelihood and severity for the rights and freedoms of natural persons, Processor shall in relation to the Company Personal Data implement appropriate technical and organizational measures to ensure a level of security appropriate to that risk, including, as appropriate, the measures referred to in Article 32(1) of the GDPR.
   4.2 In assessing the appropriate level of security, Processor shall take account in particular of the risks that are presented by Processing, in particular from a Personal Data Breach.
5. Subprocessing.
   5.1 Processor shall not appoint (or disclose any Company Personal Data to) any Subprocessor unless required or authorized by the Company.
6. Data Subject Rights.
   6.1 Taking into account the nature of the Processing, Processor shall assist the Company by implementing appropriate technical and organizational measures, insofar as this is possible, for the fulfilment of the Company obligations, as reasonably understood by Company, to respond to requests to exercise Data Subject rights under the Data Protection Laws.
   6.2 Processor shall:
      6.2.1 promptly notify Company if it receives a request from a Data Subject under any Data Protection Law in respect of Company Personal Data; and
      6.2.2 *ensure that it does not respond to that request except on the documented instructions of Company or as required by Applicable Laws to which the Processor is subject, in which case Processor shall to the extent permitted by Applicable Laws inform Company of that legal requirement before the Contracted Processor responds to the request.* (emphasis added).

7. Personal Data Breach.
    7.1 Processor shall notify Company without undue delay upon Processor becoming aware of a Personal Data Breach affecting Company Personal Data, providing Company with sufficient information to allow the Company to meet any obligations to report or inform Data Subjects of the Personal Data Breach under the Data Protection Laws.
    7.2 Processor shall co-operate with the Company and take reasonable commercial steps as are directed by Company to assist in the investigation, mitigation and remediation of each such Personal Data Breach.
8. Data Protection Impact Assessment and Prior Consultation.

    Processor shall provide reasonable assistance to the Company with any data protection impact assessments, and prior consultations with Supervising Authorities or other competent data privacy authorities, which Company reasonably considers to be required by article 35 or 36 of the GDPR or equivalent provisions of any other Data Protection Law, in each case solely in relation to Processing of Company Personal Data by, and taking into account the nature of the Processing and information available to, the Contracted Processors.
9. Deletion or Return of Company Personal Data.
    9.1 Subject to this section 9 Processor shall promptly and in any event within 10 business days of the date of cessation of any Services involving the Processing of Company Personal Data (the "Cessation Date"), delete and procure the deletion of all copies of those Company Personal Data.
    9.2 Processor shall provide written certification to Company that it has fully complied with this section 9 within 10 business days of the Cessation Date.
10. Audit Rights.
    10.1 Subject to this section 10, Processor shall make available to the Company on request all information necessary to demonstrate compliance with this Agreement, and shall allow for and contribute to audits, including inspections, by the Company or an auditor mandated by the Company in relation to the Processing of the Company Personal Data by the Contracted Processors.

10.2 Information and audit rights of the Company only arise under section 10.1 to the extent that the Agreement does not otherwise give them information and audit rights meeting the relevant requirements of Data Protection Law.

11. Data Transfer.

11.1 The Processor may not transfer or authorize the transfer of Data to countries outside the EU and/or the European Economic Area (EEA) without the prior written consent of the Company. If personal data processed under this Agreement is transferred from a country within the European Economic Area to a country outside the European Economic Area, the Parties shall ensure that the personal data are adequately protected. To achieve this, the Parties shall, unless agreed otherwise, rely on EU approved standard contractual clauses for the transfer of personal data.

12. General Terms.

12.1 Confidentiality. Each Party must keep this Agreement and information it receives about the other Party and its business in connection with this Agreement ("**Confidential Information**") confidential and must not use or disclose that Confidential Information without the prior written consent of the other Party except to the extent that:

(a) disclosure is required by law;

(b) the relevant information is already in the public domain.

12.2 Notices. All notices and communications given under this Agreement must be in writing and will be delivered personally, sent by post or sent by email to the address or email address set out in the heading of this Agreement at such other address as notified from time to time by the Parties changing address.

13. Governing Law and Jurisdiction.

13.1 This Agreement is governed by the laws of ____________.

13.2 Any dispute arising in connection with this Agreement, which the Parties will not be able to resolve amicably, will be submitted to the exclusive jurisdiction of the courts of ____________________, subject to possible appeal to _____ ________________________________.

**IN WITNESS WHEREOF**, this Agreement is entered into with effect from the date first set out below.

**Your Company**
Signature ______________________________
Name ______________________________
Title ______________________________
Date Signed ______________________________

**Processor Company**
Signature ______________________________
Name ______________________________
Title ______________________________
Date Signed ______________________________

This is a general template provided by the EU, with a couple of modifications by the authors. It is recommended that an attorney with expertise review a Data Processing Agreement and add a "Miscellaneous" section to address other related items, including specific country laws or other laws.

Noncompliance can be costly.[5] Pursuant to Article 83, "[a]ny organization that is not GDPR compliant, regardless of its size, faces a significant liability." GDPR breaks its fines down into two tiers: less severe infringements and more severe infringements, as illustrated in Table 6.1; however, member states can and do have additional penalties, including criminal penalties.

5. *Two Tiers of GDPR Fines*, EU, https://gdpr.eu/fines/ (last visited Aug. 31, 2023).

**Table 6.1** GDPR Fines

| Articles Governed | Less Severe Infringements (could result in a fine of up to 10 million Euros, or 2% of the firm's worldwide annual revenue from the preceding financial year, whichever amount is higher) | More Severe Infringements (focus on the right to privacy and the right to be forgotten; fines up to 20 million Euros or 4% of the firm's worldwide annual revenue from the preceding financial year, whichever amount is higher) |
|---|---|---|
| **Controllers and processors (Articles 8, 11, 25–39, 42, and 43)** | Organizations that collect and control data (controllers) and those that are contracted to process data (processors) must adhere to rules governing data protection, lawful basis for processing, and more. As an organization, these are the articles you need to read and adhere to. | N/A |
| **Certification bodies (Articles 42 and 43)** | Accredited bodies charged with certifying organizations must execute their evaluations and assessments without bias and via a transparent process. | N/A |
| **Monitoring bodies (Article 41)** | Bodies that have been designated to have the appropriate level of expertise must demonstrate independence and follow established procedure in handling complaints or reported infringements in an impartial and transparent manner. | N/A |

| Articles Governed | Less Severe Infringements (could result in a fine of up to 10 million Euros, or 2% of the firm's worldwide annual revenue from the preceding financial year, whichever amount is higher) | More Severe Infringements (focus on the right to privacy and the right to be forgotten; fines up to 20 million Euros or 4% of the firm's worldwide annual revenue from the preceding financial year, whichever amount is higher) |
|---|---|---|
| **The basic principles for processing (Articles 5, 6 and 9)** | N/A | Data processing must be done in a lawful, fair, and transparent manner. It has to be collected and processed for a specific purpose, be kept accurate and up to date, and be processed in a manner that ensures its security. Organizations are only allowed to process data if they meet one of the six lawful bases listed in Article 6. In addition, certain types of personal data, including racial origin, political opinions, religious beliefs, trade union membership, sexual orientation, and health or biometric data are prohibited except under specific circumstances. |
| **The conditions for consent (Article 7)** | N/A | When an organization's data processing is justified based on the person's consent, that organization needs to have the documentation to prove it. |

| Articles Governed | Less Severe Infringements (could result in a fine of up to 10 million Euros, or 2% of the firm's worldwide annual revenue from the preceding financial year, whichever amount is higher) | More Severe Infringements (focus on the right to privacy and the right to be forgotten; fines up to 20 million Euros or 4% of the firm's worldwide annual revenue from the preceding financial year, whichever amount is higher) |
|---|---|---|
| **The data subjects' rights (Articles 12–22)** | N/A | Individuals have a right to know what data an organization is collecting and what they are doing with it. They also have a right to obtain a copy of the data collected, to have this data corrected, and, in certain cases, the right to have this data be erased. People also have a right to transfer their data to another organization. |
| **The transfer of data to an international organization or a recipient in a third country (Articles 44–49)** | N/A | Before an organization transfers any personal data to a third country or international organization, the European Commission must decide that that country or organization ensures an adequate level of protection. The transfers themselves must be safeguarded. |

Additionally, under Chapter IX, EU member states may also adopt individual country laws that accord with GDPR, and any violations of these national laws also potentially subject the controller or processor to fines. Moreover, Article 82 provides data subjects (i.e., individuals) the ability to seek compensation from organizations that cause damages connected to GDPR violations.

Vetting third parties is also critical. As the EU suggests,

> Many companies use third parties, like email or cloud storage services, to handle their data. While this can be helpful in adhering to the GDPR if the third party has a higher technological capacity, it does not absolve the hiring organization (i.e., the controller) from ensuring that personal data is processed in accordance with the GDPR. Unless the controller can clearly demonstrate that it was "not in any way responsible for the event giving rise to the damage," it will be fully liable for any infringement caused by a noncompliant third party.[6]

Let's consider an individual member state. Ireland houses a lot of data, and while GDPR could be adopted "as is" by individual member states, there are certain aspects that an individual country could give further effect in a national law.[7] In Ireland, further effect was given to GDPR through the Data Protection Act 2018, and the Irish Supervisory Authority is the Office of the Data Protection Commissioner, aka Data Protection Commission (DPC).[8] As Amnesty International dubbed it, the DPC "is a vital data protection regulator, with a unique responsibility."[9] Another unique aspect of Irish fines related to the Data Protection Act 2018, its adaptation of GDPR, is that the "penalty is described as not insurable."[10] A case in point is the recent investigation of a complaint, finding, and preliminary decision, which was handed to LinkedIn and its parent company Microsoft in spring 2023.

In April 2023, the IDPC provided LinkedIn with a nonpublic preliminary draft decision that proposed a fine. After review and analysis, [Microsoft] increased its existing reserve for the matter and, based on current exchange rates, took a charge of approximately $425 million in the fourth quarter of fiscal year 2023.

---

6. *Data Controller's Responsibility*, EU, https://gdpr.eu/fines/ (last visited Aug. 31, 2023) (noting that this section appears at the bottom of the webpage).

7. *See* www.dataprotection.ie (last visited Aug. 31, 2023).

8. *Id.*

9. *See* https://www.amnesty.org/en/latest/news/2023/06/ireland-draconian-law-to-make-data-protection-procedures-confidential/ (June 28, 2023).

10. Terry Gangcuangco, *Microsoft Faces "Uninsurable" GDPR Penalty,* Insurance News (June 5, 2023), https://www.insurancebusinessmag.com/us/news/breaking-news/microsoft-faces-uninsurable-gdpr-penalty-448121.aspx.

Microsoft, which has all intentions to respond to the draft decision, is planning to dispute the legal basis for the proposed fine, as well as the amount. The tech giant added that it will continue to defend its compliance with GDPR.

Meanwhile, it was noted that there is no set timeline as to when a final decision will be issued by the IDPC. "However, after receiving a final decision, Microsoft will consider all legal options and intends to defend itself vigorously in this matter,"[11] asserted the global corporation.

As Aon's report "The Price of Data Security" indicates, there are 18 countries where GDPR fines are not insurable—Austria, Belgium, Bulgaria, Cyprus, Denmark, Finland, France, Ireland, Italy, Latvia, Luxembourg, Malta, Portugal, Romania, Slovenia, Spain, Switzerland, and the UK.[12] Hence, because LinkedIn's case is in Ireland, it is not insurable. This leads us to NIST and ISO's framework for cybersecurity risks and enterprise risk management across an organization and why cybersecurity insurance is a consideration often utilized as a financial risk mitigation measure.

## CSF 2.0 and Its Application to the Concept of "Left of Bang"

"The 'Left of Bang' approach requires organizations to develop better situational awareness through an understanding of cyber risks."[13] In other words, organizations must be proactive through compliance and utilizing a protection, detection, and correction approach to cybersecurity, instead of waiting for an event while being knowingly exposed and therefore having to be completely reactive. A great resource to utilize is CSF 2.0, the draft of which was published on August 8, 2023, with final comments due by November 4, 2023.[14] As stated on its website, "[t]he NIST Cybersecurity Framework was intended to be a living document that is refined,

---

11. *Irish Data Regulator Could Impose around $425m Fine on LinkedIn,* VERDICT (June 2, 2023), https://www.verdict.co.uk/idpc-fine-on-linkedin/.

12. *See* THE PRICE OF DATA SECURITY (May 2020), https://www.dlapiper.com/-/media/project/dlapiper-tenant/dlapiper/pdf/a-guide-to-the-insurability-of-gdpr-fines-across-europe.pdf (last visited Aug. 31, 2023).

13. *See* https://augustagrp.com/left-of-bang-cyber-3 (last visited Aug. 31, 2023).

14. *The NIST Cybersecurity Framework 2.0,* NIST (Aug. 8, 2023), https://csrc.nist.gov/pubs/cswp/29/the-nist-cybersecurity-framework-20/ipd.

improved, and evolves over time. These updates help the Framework keep pace with technology and threat trends, integrate lessons learned, and move best practice to common practice. NIST initially produced the Framework in 2014 and updated it in April 2018 with CSF 1.1."[15] A notable addition to the CSF is the term "govern," which is represented in an inner circle, while the five external circle terms—"identify, protect, detect, respond, recover"—remain the same (see Figure 6.1).[16]

**Figure 6.1** NIST Cybersecurity Framework

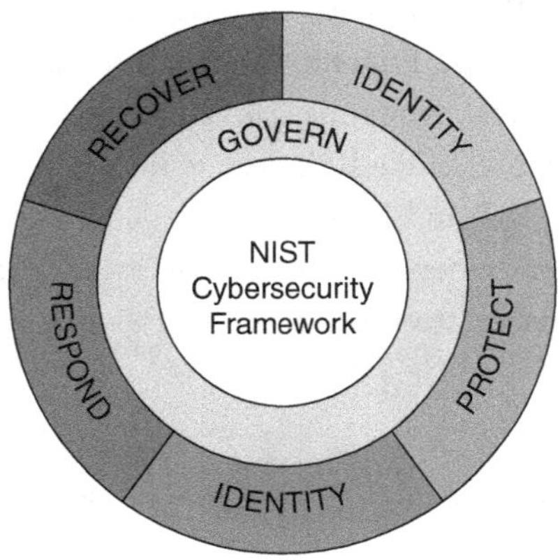


This begs the question—how is "govern" defined? NIST breaks it down as follows:

- **Function–Govern (GV).** Establish and monitor the organization's cybersecurity risk management strategy, expectations, and policy.
- Category
  - **Organizational Context (GV.OC).** The circumstances—mission; stakeholder expectations; and legal, regulatory, and

15. *See* https://www.nist.gov/cyberframework/updating-nist-cybersecurity-framework-journey-csf-20 (last visited Aug. 29, 2023).

16. *Cybersecurity Framework (CSF)*, NIST, https://csrc.nist.gov/Projects/cybersecurity-framework/Filters#/csf/filters (last visited Aug. 29, 2023) (stating, "[a]spects related to the presentation and functionality of this Tool are still under development. Informative References will be added once CSF 2.0 is finalized in early 2024, which will help to show the connection between the CSF and other cybersecurity frameworks, standards, guidelines, and resources. Since CSF 2.0 Implementation Examples and Informative References will be updated more frequently than the rest of the Core, they will be published and maintained online only.").

contractual requirements—surrounding the organization's cybersecurity risk management decisions are understood (formerly ID.BE).

- **Risk Management Strategy (GV.RM).** The organization's priorities, constraints, risk tolerance and appetite statements, and assumptions are established, communicated, and used to support operational risk decisions (formerly ID.RM).
    - **GV.RM-01.** Risk management objectives are established and agreed to be organizational stakeholders (formerly ID.RM-01).
    - **GV.RM-02.** Risk appetite and risk tolerance statements are determined, communicated, and maintained (formerly ID.RM-02, ID.RM-03).
        - **Ex1.** Update near-term and long-term cybersecurity risk management objectives as part of annual strategic planning and when major changes occur.
        - **Ex2.** Establish measurable objectives for cybersecurity risk management (e.g., manage the quality of the user training, ensure adequate risk protections for industrial control systems).
        - **Ex3.** Senior leaders agree about cybersecurity objectives and use them for measuring and managing risk performance.
    - **GV.RM-03.** Enterprise risk management processes include cybersecurity risk management activities and outcomes (formerly ID.GV-04).
        - **Ex1. Aggregate and manage cybersecurity risks alongside other enterprise risks (e.g., compliance, financial, and regulatory)** (emphasis added).
        - **Ex2.** Include cybersecurity risk managers in enterprise risk management planning.
        - **Ex3.** Establish criteria for escalating cybersecurity risks within enterprise risk management.
    - **GV.RM-04.** Strategic direction that describes appropriate risk response options is established and communicated.
        - **Ex1.** Specify criteria for accepting and avoiding cybersecurity risk for various classifications of data.
        - **Ex2.** Determine whether to purchase cybersecurity insurance.

- **Ex3.** Document conditions under which shared responsibility models are acceptable (e.g., outsourcing certain cybersecurity functions, having a third party perform financial transactions on behalf of the organization, using public cloud services).[17]

And, the list goes on. One item that permeates through the current and DRAFT CSF is the need for effective communication that is memorialized in a standardized method (e.g., diagrams), and needs to be addressed on a variety of fronts (e.g., third parties, clients/customers, internally amongst individuals and divisions).[18] "ISO 27001 and NIST CSF are complementary frameworks based on similar risk management processes."[19] Like the United States' NIST standards, which assist public and private organizations implement a framework to protect the confidentiality, integrity, and availability of its data, ISO's goals are the same. Presently, 114 controls are outlined in ISO 27001, which are parsed out into 14 sections.[20]

The technical, administrative, and physical safeguard requirements of ISO mirror those of NIST. One control that stands out is A.6.2 Mobile Devices and Teleworking, and its objective "[t]o ensure the security of the teleworking and use of mobile devices."[21] Specifically,

- A.6.2.1 Mobile device policy. A policy and supporting security measures shall be adopted to manage the risks introduced by using mobile devices.
- A.6.2.2 Telworking [sic]. A policy and supporting security measures shall be implemented to protect information access, process or stored at teleworking sites.[22]

---

17. *Id.*

18. *Id.*

19. *ISO 27001 vs. NIST Cybersecurity Framework*, ONETRUST, https://www.onetrust.com/blog/iso-27001-vs-nist-cybersecurity-framework/#:~:text=ISO%2027001%20and%20NIST%20CSF%20are%20complementary%20frameworks%20based%20on,Monitor%20their%20performance (last visited Aug. 29, 2023).

20. ISO 27001—INTERNATIONAL STANDARDS ORGANIZATION SECURITY CONTROL FRAMEWORK, https://www.cssia.org/wp-content/uploads/2020/01/ISO_27001_Standard.pdf (Jan. 2020).

21. *Id.*

22. *Id.*

One critical area related to teleworking and mobile device utilization is network security. By now, everyone should appreciate, as the U.S. National Security Agency (NSA) does, that "malicious techniques used to target each technology and provides specific recommendations, such as avoiding public Wi-Fi and instead using a personal or corporate mobile hotspot with strong authentication and encryption."[23] Likewise, home networks are equally vulnerable. In February 2023, NSA published *Best Practices for Securing Your Home Network* and included the following considerations for protecting "personal, private, and confidential information" and practicing cyber hygiene to mitigate at-home risks:[24]

- Upgrade and update all equipment and software regularly, including routing devices.
- Exercise secure habits by backing up your data and disconnecting devices when connections are not needed.
- Limit administration to the internal network only.

See Figure 6.2.

Of the "best practices" mentioned by the NSA, *Securing Routing Devices and Keeping Them Up to Date* is one not to overlook.[25] NSA's elaboration follows:

> Your Internet Service Provider (ISP) may provide a modem/router as part of your service contract. To maximize administrative control over the routing and wireless features of your home network, consider using a personally owned routing device that connects to the ISP-provided modem/router. In addition, use modern router features to create a separate wireless network for guests, for network separation from your more trusted and private devices.

23. *NSA Issues Guidance on Securing Wireless Devices in Public Settings,* Nat'l Security Agency (July 29, 2021), https://www.nsa.gov/Press-Room/News-Highlights/Article/Article/2711968/nsa-issues-guidance-on-securing-wireless-devices-in-public-settings/#:~:text=NSA%20lists%20malicious%20techniques%20used,with%20strong%20authentication%20and%20encryption.

24. *Best Practices for Securing Your Home Network,* Nat'l Security Agency (Feb. 2023), https://www.nsa.gov/Press-Room/News-Highlights/Article/Article/3304674/nsa-releases-best-practices-for-securing-your-home-network/.

25. *Id.* at 2.

**Figure 6.2** Best Practices for Securing Your Home Network

National Security Agency | Cybersecurity Information Sheet

## Best Practices for Securing Your Home Network

### Executive summary

Don't be a victim! Malicious cyber actors may leverage your home network to gain access to personal, private, and confidential information. Help protect yourself, your family, and your work by practicing cybersecurity-aware behaviors, observing some basic configuration guidelines, and implementing the following mitigations on your home network, including:

- Upgrade and update all equipment and software regularly, including routing devices
- Exercise secure habits by backing up your data and disconnecting devices when connections are not needed
- Limit administration to the internal network only

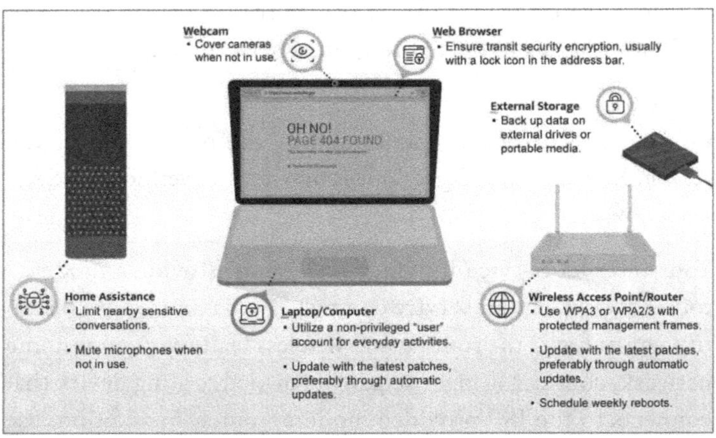


Your router is the gateway into your home network. Without proper security and patching, it is more likely to be compromised, which can lead to the compromise of other devices on the network as well. To minimize vulnerabilities and improve security, the routing devices on your home network should be updated to the latest patches, preferably through automatic updates. These devices should also be replaced when they reach end-of-life (EOL) for support. This ensures that all devices can continue to be updated and patched as vulnerabilities are discovered.

Additionally, Wi-Fi Protected Access 3 (WPA3) or WPA2 with a strong passphrase should be selected. Most ISP providers have a WPA2/3 option, which allows newer devices to use WPA3, which is more secure while still allowing older devices to utilize WPA2.[26]

By adhering to NIST and ISO frameworks, as well as the HIPAA Security Rule and related laws such as GDPR, persons can show that they are acting in good faith to meet the requisite regulatory standards. Staying abreast of best practices and disseminating them to workforce members—both in office and remote—is a best practice, along with an annual risk analysis performed by a qualified third party, to ensure that privacy and security regulatory requirements are being met.

26. *Id.* at 3.

# CHAPTER 7

# Privacy Shields

"If you lose your integrity, you will also lose your identity, your sensitivity and your dignity. Integrity is honesty, modesty and security in all kinds of weather. It should be our priority."

—Israelmore Ayivor

Integrity is not an amorphous concept in terms of data privacy and security. It is one of the three core requirements—confidentiality, integrity, and availability. These core requirements are set forth in the NIST and ISO standards and they apply to the Privacy Shields.[1]

## What Are Privacy Shields and Personal Data Transfers?

The term "Privacy Shields" refers to the EU–U.S. Privacy Shield, United Kingdom–U.S. Privacy Shield, and the Swiss–U.S. Privacy Shield.[2]

> The EU–U.S. Data Privacy Framework (EU–U.S. DPF), the UK Extension to the EU–U.S. Data Privacy Framework (UK Extension to the EU–U.S. DPF), and the Swiss–U.S. Data Privacy Framework (Swiss–U.S. DPF) were respectively developed in furtherance of transatlantic commerce by the U.S. Department of Commerce and the European Commission, the UK Government, and the Swiss Federal Administration to provide U.S. organizations with reliable mechanisms for personal data transfers to the United States from the European Union / European Economic Area, the United Kingdom (and Gibraltar), and

1. *See* https://www.itgovernanceusa.com/iso27001-and-nist (last visited Aug. 17, 2023).

2. *See* https://www.dataprivacyframework.gov/s/ (last visited Aug. 17, 2023).

> Switzerland while ensuring data protection that is consistent with EU, UK, and Swiss law.[3]

Designed by the U.S. Department of Commerce (DOC) and the European Commission (EC), and launched in July 2016,[4] the *EU-US Privacy Shield Framework* "provide[s] companies on both sides of the Atlantic with a mechanism to comply with EU data protection requirements when transferring personal data from the European Union to the United States in support of transatlantic commerce."[5] The ride has not been smooth, and there was an approximate three-year delay between the repealing of the Privacy Shield and when the Privacy Shield was reinstated, with some alterations in July 2023 due to *Data Protection Commission v. Facebook Ireland, Schrems* (*Schrems II*).[6] On March 25, 2022, the White House announced that the EU and the U.S. committed to a revised Trans-Atlantic Data Privacy Framework to foster and protect trans-Atlantic data flows and to address the concerns raised by the EU's Court of Justice in *Schrems II*.[7] "On July 10, 2023, the EU adopted an adequacy decision for the EU-U.S. DPF after determining that the additional safeguards included in EO 14086 and the EU-U.S. DPF provide an adequate level of protection for personal data transferred from the European Union."[8] The requirements are detailed later in this chapter.

---

3. *See* https://www.dataprivacyframework.gov/s/program-overview (last visited Aug. 17, 2023).

4. Press Release, European Commission, European Commission Launches EU-U.S. Privacy Shield: Stronger Protection for Transatlantic Data Flows (July 12, 2016), https://ec.europa.eu/commission/presscorner/detail/en/IP_16_2461.

5. *EU–U.S. Privacy Shield*, U.S. Dep't of Com., https://www.commerce.gov/tags/eu-us-privacy-shield (last visited Aug. 17, 2023).

6. Data Protection Commission v. Facebook Ireland, Schrems, Case C-311/18 (2020) (*Schrems II*).

7. Press Release, The White House, FACT SHEET: United States and European Commission Announce Trans-Atlantic Data Privacy Framework (Mar. 25, 2022), https://www.whitehouse.gov/briefing-room/statements-releases/2022/03/25/fact-sheet-united-states-and-european-commission-announce-trans-atlantic-data-privacy-framework/; *see also Schrems II*, ¶ 105 (noting that "the assessment of the level of protection afforded in the context of such a transfer must," inter alia, consider the relevant laws of a third country "as regards any access by the public authorities of that third country to the personal data transferred").

8. *Data Privacy Framework Program Launches New Website Enabling U.S. Companies to Participate in Cross-Border Data Transfers* U.S. Dep't of Com. (July 17, 2023), https://www.commerce.gov/news/press-releases/2023/07/data-privacy-framework-program

One item to consider is medical data, especially in the context of international health research, treatment, and pharmaceutical/medical device discovery, which in turn subjects the data and the parties to HIPAA.[9] At least one article has argued that "the [Privacy] Shield is ill-suited to support complex health studies [and] [i]ts legitimacy is in question under both EU and US law, and terms are too restrictive for the variety of exchanges underlying research, treatment, and care."[10] In 2022, the European Commission issued 2022/0140(COD) Proposal for a Regulation of the European Parliament and of the Council on the European Health Data Space (EHDS), in which it identified its impetus—to address challenges associated with electronic health data, "including accessing and transmitting their electronic data nationally and cross-borders . . . despite the provisions of Regulation (EU) 2016/679 [GDPR]."[11] Prior to EHDS, a 2011 directive, 2011/24/EU (specifically Article 14), was the initial reference to eHealth in EU legislation.[12]

> However, as stated in the impact assessment accompanying this EHDS Regulation, the relevant provisions of CBHC Directive are voluntary in nature. This partly explains why this aspect of the Directive has shown limited effectiveness in supporting natural persons' control over their personal electronic health data at national and cross-border level and very low effectiveness on secondary uses of electronic health data. The COVID-19 pandemic has revealed the urgent need and the high potential for interoperability and harmonisation, building upon existing technical expertise at national level. At the same time, digital health products and services, including telemedicine, have become an intrinsic part of the delivery of healthcare.
>
> . . .

-launches-new-website-enabling-us#:~:text=On%20July%2010%2C%202023%2C%20the,transferred%20from%20the%20European%20Union.

9. Laura Bradford, Mateo Aboy & Kathleen Liddell, International Transfers of Health Data between the EU and USA: A Sector-Specific Approach for the USA to Ensure an 'Adequate' Level of Protection 7(1) J. Law Biosc. (Jan./Dec. 2020), https://www.ncbi.nlm.nih.gov/pmc/articles/PMC8249089/.

10. *Id.*

11. EC, 2022/0140-COD) (3.5.2022), https://eur-lex.europa.eu/procedure/EN/2022_140.

12. *Id.*

> Cross-border exchange of electronic health data is to a certain extent addressed in the CBHC Directive in particular in its Article 14 on the eHealth Network. Established in 2011, it is a voluntary body at European level composed of digital health experts of all Member States with Iceland and Norway. They are working to promote EU-wide interoperability of electronic health data and to develop guidelines, such as semantic and technical standards, datasets and descriptions of infrastructures. The evaluation of the digital aspects of CBHC Directive noted the voluntary nature of this work and the guidelines. This explains why they have had a rather limited impact on supporting natural persons' access to and control over their electronic health data. The EHDS aims to address these issues.[13]

While the EDHS augments GDPR, EU Regulation 2017/745 (Medical Devices Regulation), EU Regulation 2017/746 (in vitro diagnostic medical devices (In Vitro Diagnostics Regulation), the proposed Artificial Intelligence Act, the proposed Data Governance Act, Directive 2016/1148 on security of network and information systems (NIS Directive),[14] it is also relevant to the Privacy Shield because the U.S. Federal Trade Commission has jurisdiction over violations related to consumers' health data, as well as inadequate cyber safeguards, which impact the privacy and the security of the data. Electronic Health Record vendors, as well as controllers and processers as defined in GDPR, and those utilizing the data for secondary uses, should read EDHS closely. This brings us to the *Schrems II* decision.

---

13. *Id.*

14. Regulation (EU) 2017/745 of the European Parliament and of the Council of 5 April 2017 on medical devices, amending Directive 2001/83/EC, Regulation (EC) No. 178/2002 and Regulation (EC) No. 1223/2009 and repealing Council Directives 90/385/EEC and 93/42/EEC (OJ L 117, 5.5.2017, p. 1–175); Regulation (EU) 2017/746 of the European Parliament and of the Council of 5 April 2017 on in vitro diagnostic medical devices and repealing Directive 98/79/EC and Commission Decision 2010/227/EU (OJ L 117, 5.5.2017, p. 176–332); Proposal for a Regulation laying down harmonized rules on artificial intelligence (Artificial Intelligence Act), COM/2021/206 final (last visited Aug. 20, 2023); Proposal for a Regulation on European data governance (Data Governance Act) COM/2020/767 final; Directive (EU) 2016/1148 of the European Parliament and of the Council of 6 July 2016 concerning measures for a high common level of security of network and information systems across the Union (OJ L 194, 19.7.2016, p. 1–30).

## *Data Protection Commission v. Facebook Ireland, Schrems (Schrems II)*

Before delving into *Schrems II*, addressing the precursors is mandatory. *Maximillian Schrems v. Data Protection Commissioner* (*Schrems I*),[15] which is a seminal international privacy case that arose out of a 2013 complaint against Facebook Ireland, Ltd. by Mr. Schrems, an Austrian privacy advocate.[16] The complaint alleged that the transfer of data (both his individually, as well as that of EU citizens in general) from Ireland, where Facebook is incorporated to the United States, was in violation of the Safe Harbor Framework, which governed data transfers between the EU and the United States. Paragraph 35 of the Court of Justice of the European Union's (CJEU) Opinion states:

> The High Court further observes that in his action Mr Schrems in reality raises the legality of the safe harbour regime which was established by Decision 2000/520 and gives rise to the decision at issue in the main proceedings. Thus, even though Mr Schrems has not formally contested the validity of either Directive 95/46 or Decision 2000/520, the question is raised, according to the High Court, as to whether, on account of Article 25(6) of Directive 95/46, the Commissioner was bound by the Commission's finding in Decision 2000/520 that the United States ensures an adequate level of protection or whether Article 8 of the Charter authorised the Commissioner to break free, if appropriate, from such a finding.[17]

Resultantly, the CJEU's October 6, 2015, opinion led to the invalidation of the previous EU–U.S. data-sharing provision.

Fast forward ahead to July 16, 2020. In *Schrems II*, the CJEU "invalidated the EU-U.S. Privacy Shield, finding that U.S. surveillance laws do not afford EU data subjects adequate levels of protection under the European Union's Charter of Fundamental Rights (the "Charter") and General Data Protection Regulation (GDPR). Specifically, the court found

---

15. Maximillian Schrems v. Data Protection Comm'r, 62014 C.J. 0362 (Oct. 6, 2015) (*Schrems I*).

16. *See* https://eur-lex.europa.eu/legal-content/EN/TXT/?uri=CELEX%3A62014CJ0362 (Oct. 6, 2015).

17. *Id.*

that section 702 of the Foreign Intelligence Surveillance Act (FISA) and Executive Order 12,333 are overly broad and lack sufficient redress for EU data subjects."[18] In essence, leaving nearly 5,000 U.S. and EU companies without an alternative data transfer framework[19] until July 2023, as set forth next.

## Status of the Privacy Shield between the United States, the European Union, Switzerland, and the United Kingdom Post *Schrems II*

The U.S. DOC sums it up succinctly, so there is no need to reinvent the wheel. The status follows:

> Effective as of July 17, 2023, eligible organizations in the United States that wish to self-certify their compliance pursuant to the UK Extension to the EU-U.S. DPF may do so; however, personal data cannot be received from the United Kingdom and Gibraltar in reliance on the UK Extension to the EU-U.S. DPF before the date that the adequacy regulations implementing the data bridge for the UK Extension to the EU-U.S. DPF enter into force. The data bridge will enable the transfer of UK and Gibraltar personal data to participating organizations consistent with UK law.
>
> The effective date of the Swiss-U.S. DPF Principles, including the Supplemental Principles and Annex I of the Principles is July 17, 2023; however, personal data cannot be received from Switzerland in reliance on the Swiss-U.S. DPF until the date of entry into force of Switzerland's recognition of adequacy for the Swiss-U.S. DPF. The recognition of adequacy will enable the transfer of Swiss personal data to participating organizations consistent with Swiss law.

---

18. *National Security Law—Surveillance—Court of Justice of the European Union Invalidates the EU-U.S. Privacy Shield,* at 1 (Feb. 2021) https://harvardlawreview.org/wp-content/uploads/2021/02/134-Harv.-L.-Rev.-1567.pdf.

19. *Id.*

The Data Privacy Framework (DPF) program, which is administered by the International Trade Administration (ITA) within the U.S. Department of Commerce, enables eligible U.S.-based organizations to self-certify their compliance pursuant to the EU-U.S. DPF and, as applicable, the UK Extension to the EU-U.S. DPF, and/or the Swiss-U.S. DPF. To participate in the DPF program, a U.S.-based organization is required to self-certify to the ITA via the Department's Data Privacy Framework (DPF) program website (*i.e.*, this website) and publicly commit to comply with the DPF Principles. While the decision by an eligible U.S.-based organization to self-certify its compliance pursuant to and participate in the relevant part(s) of the DPF program is voluntary, effective compliance upon self-certification is compulsory. Once such an organization self-certifies to the ITA and publicly declares its commitment to adhere to the DPF Principles that commitment is enforceable under U.S. law.

Organizations that only wish to self-certify their compliance pursuant to the EU-U.S. DPF and/or the Swiss-U.S. DPF may do so; however, organizations that wish to participate in the UK Extension to the EU-U.S. DPF must participate in the EU-U.S. DPF. Such organizations' commitment to comply with the EU-U.S. DPF Principles with regard to transfers of personal data from the European Union and, as applicable, the United Kingdom (and Gibraltar), and/or the Swiss-U.S. DPF Principles with regard to transfers from Switzerland must be reflected in their self-certification submissions to the ITA, and at appropriate times in their relevant privacy policies. Organizations that self-certified their compliance pursuant to the EU-U.S. Privacy Shield that wish to enjoy the benefits of participating in the EU-U.S. DPF must comply with the EU-U.S. DPF Principles; and organizations that self-certified their compliance pursuant to the Swiss-U.S. Privacy Shield that wish to enjoy the benefits of participating in the Swiss-U.S. DPF must comply with the Swiss-U.S. DPF Principles.

To rely on the EU-U.S. DPF and, as applicable, the UK Extension to the EU-U.S. DPF, and/or the Swiss-U.S. DPF for transfers of personal data from the European Union and, as

> applicable, the United Kingdom (and Gibraltar), and/or Switzerland an organization must not only self-certify its adherence to the DPF Principles to the ITA, but also both be placed and remain on the Data Privacy Framework List. The ITA will update the Data Privacy Framework List on the basis of annual re-certification submissions made by participating organizations and by removing organizations when they voluntarily withdraw, fail to complete the annual re-certification in accordance with the ITA's procedures, or are found to persistently fail to comply. The ITA will also maintain and make available to the public an authoritative record of U.S. organizations that have been removed from the Data Privacy Framework List and will identify the reason each organization was removed. The aforementioned authoritative list and record will remain available to the public on the Department's DPF program website. Any organization removed from the Data Privacy Framework List must cease making claims that it participates in or complies with the EU-U.S. DPF and, as applicable, the UK Extension to the EU-U.S. DPF, and/or the Swiss-U.S. DPF and that it may receive personal information pursuant to same. Such an organization must nevertheless continue to apply the DPF Principles to personal information that it received while it participated in the EU-U.S. DPF and, as applicable, the UK Extension to the EU-U.S. DPF, and/or the Swiss-U.S. DPF for as long as it retains such personal information.[20]

Given the prerequisite that organizations wishing to participate in the UK Extension *must* participate in the EU–U.S. Privacy Shield, a prudent first step would be to participate in the EU–U.S. Privacy Shield. This leads us to the core requirements in several key areas as reflected in Table 7.1.[21]

---

20. *See* https://www.dataprivacyframework.gov/s/program-overview (last visited Aug. 17, 2023).

21. *See* https://www.dataprivacyframework.gov/s/key-requirements (last visited Aug. 17, 2023).

Table 7.1

| Category | Considerations |
|---|---|
| **Informing individuals about data processing** | • A participating organization must include in its privacy policy a declaration of the participating organization's commitment to comply with the DPF Principles, so that the commitment becomes enforceable under U.S. law.<br>• A participating organization's privacy policy must include a link to the U.S. Department of Commerce's DPF program website and a link to or the web address for the relevant website or complaint submission form of the independent recourse mechanisms that is available to investigate individual complaints brought under the DPF Principles.<br>• A participating organization must inform individuals of their rights to access their personal data, the requirement to disclose personal information in response to lawful request by public authorities, which enforcement authority has jurisdiction over the participating organization's compliance with the DPF Principles, and the participating organization's liability in cases of onward transfer of data to third parties. |
| **Providing free and accessible dispute resolution** | • Individuals may bring a complaint directly to a participating organization, and the participant must respond to the individual within 45 days.<br>• Participating organizations must provide, at no cost to the individual, an independent recourse mechanism by which each individual's complaints and disputes can be investigated and expeditiously resolved.<br>• If an individual submits a complaint to a data protection authority (DPA) in the European Union / European Economic Area, the United Kingdom (and/or, as applicable, Gibraltar) or Switzerland, the U.S. Department of Commerce's International Trade Administration (ITA) has committed to receive, review, and undertake best efforts to facilitate resolution of the complaint and to respond to the DPA within 90 days.<br>• Participating organizations must also commit to binding arbitration at the request of the individual to address any complaint that has not been resolved by other recourse and enforcement mechanisms. |
| **Cooperating with the U.S. Department of Commerce** | • Participating organizations must respond promptly to inquiries and requests by the ITA for information relating to the EU–U.S Data Privacy Framework (EU–U.S. DPF) and, as applicable the UK Extension to the EU–U.S. DPF, and/or the Swiss–U.S. Data Privacy Framework (Swiss–U.S. DPF). |

| Category | Considerations |
|---|---|
| **Maintaining data integrity and purpose limitation** | • Participating organizations must limit personal information to the information relevant for the purposes of processing.<br>• Participating organizations must comply with the data retention provision. |
| **Ensuring accountability for data transferred to third parties** | To transfer personal information to a third party acting as a controller, a participating organization must:<br>• Comply with the Notice and Choice Principles; and<br>• Enter into a contract with the third-party controller that provides that such data may only be processed for limited and specified purposes consistent with the consent provided by the individual and that the recipient will provide the same level of protection as the DPF Principles and will notify the organization if it makes a determination that it can no longer meet this obligation. The contract shall provide that when such a determination is made the third-party controller ceases processing or takes other reasonable and appropriate steps to remediate.<br>To transfer personal data to a third party acting as an agent, a participating organization must:<br>• Transfer such data only for limited and specified purposes;<br>• Ascertain that the agent is obligated to provide at least the same level of privacy protection as is required by the DPF Principles;<br>• Take reasonable and appropriate steps to ensure that the agent effectively processes the personal information transferred in a manner consistent with the organization's obligations under the DPF Principles;<br>• Require the agent to notify the organization if it makes a determination that it can no longer meet its obligation to provide the same level of protection as is required by the DPF Principles;<br>• Upon notice, take reasonable and appropriate steps to stop and remediate unauthorized processing; and<br>• Provide a summary or a representative copy of the relevant privacy provisions of its contract with that agent to the U.S. Department of Commerce upon request. |
| **Transparency related to enforcement actions** | Participating organizations must make public any relevant DPF-related sections of any compliance or assessment report submitted to the Federal Trade Commission (FTC) or the U.S. Department of Transportation if the organization becomes subject to an FTC or court order based on noncompliance. |

| Category | Considerations |
|---|---|
| **Ensuring commitments are kept as long as data is held** | If an organization leaves the relevant part(s) of the DPF program, it must annually affirm to the ITA its commitment to apply the DPF Principles to information received under the relevant part(s) of the DPF program if it chooses to keep such data; otherwise, it must provide "adequate" protection for the information by another authorized means. |

To be clear, while there are benefits to voluntarily self-certifying initially and subsequently on an annual basis to the DOC's International Trade Administration (ITA), there are other considerations, although other regulatory bodies such as the FTC, DOT, DOJ, SEC, and HHS already have jurisdiction over noncompliance and material misstatements regarding cybersecurity standards (e.g., NIST and ISO) and compliance with HIPAA, GDPR, and other laws, the self-certification "commitment is enforceable under U.S. law by the relevant enforcement authority (i.e., by the Federal Trade Commission (FTC), the U.S. Department of Transportation (DOT), or other relevant government body."[22] In essence, there are eight steps to self-certification:

1. **Confirm your organization's eligibility to participate in the DPF program.** "Only U.S. legal entities subject to the jurisdiction of the Federal Trade Commission (FTC) or the U.S. Department of Transportation (DOT) are currently eligible to participate in the DPF program."[23] Notably, persons that create, receive, maintain, and/or transmit consumer individually identifiable health information (IIHI) or if a company (domestic or foreign) is registered with the SEC, then the reach is there for enforcement by other U.S. government agencies.[24]

22. *See* https://www.dataprivacyframework.gov/s/article/How-to-Join-the-Data-Privacy-Framework-DPF-Program-part-1-dpf (last visited Aug. 17, 2023).

23. *Id.*

24. Rachel V. Rose, Ted Dziekanowski & Andy Watkin-Child, *SEC Cybersecurity Rule Leans on Materiality and Reasonableness,* Bloomberg Law (Aug. 18, 2023) https://news.bloomberglaw.com/us-law-week/sec-cybersecurity-rule-leans-on-materiality-and-reasonableness; *see also* Rachel V. Rose & Bob Chaput, *The Nexus between the SEC's Final Rule and the Health Care Industry,* Health Law Weekly (Aug. 4, 2023), https://www.americanhealthlaw.org/content-library/health-law-weekly/article/ffb0b8d8-43d9-4983-855e-806ec6b2b70a/the-nexus-between-the-sec-s-final-rule-and-the-hea.

2. **Develop a DPF-compliant privacy policy statement.** Your organization must develop a DPF-compliant privacy policy before submitting its initial self-certification to the ITA.[25]
3. **Ensure that your organization has an appropriate independent recourse mechanism in place for each type of personal data covered by its self-certification**. Under the Recourse, Enforcement, and Liability Principle, self-certifying organizations must make an independent recourse mechanism available to investigate unresolved complaints brought under the DPF Principles and provide appropriate recourse free of charge to the affected individual.
4. **Make the required contribution for the annex I binding arbitration mechanism.**
5. **Ensure that your organization's verification mechanism is in place.** Your organization must have procedures in place for verifying that the attestations and assertions that it makes about its DPF privacy practices are true, and those privacy practices have been implemented as represented and in accordance with the DPF Principles.
6. **Designate a contact within your organization regarding DPF compliance.** Your organization is required to provide a contact for the handling of complaints, access requests, and any other issues concerning your organization's compliance with the EU–U.S. DPF and, as applicable, the UK Extension to the EU–U.S. DPF, and/or the Swiss–U.S. DPF. This contact can be either the corporate officer that is certifying your organization's compliance with the DPF Principles, or another official within your organization, such as a chief privacy officer. Under the DPF Principles, organizations must respond to individuals within 45 days of receiving a complaint.
7. **Review the information required to self-certify.** Prior to submitting a self-certification via the DPF program website (i.e., this website), your organization should review and compile the information required as part of the ITA's online self-certification process.

25. *See* https://www.dataprivacyframework.gov/s/article/FAQs-Privacy-Policy-1-5-dpf (last visited Aug. 17, 2023).

8. **Submit your organization's self-certification to the ITA.** Click on the "self-certify" link on this website to create a profile and submit your organization's self-certification. Submission of your organization's self-certification will also require payment of a self-certification processing fee. The self-certification processing fee is part of the ITA's cost recovery program to support the operation of the DPF program. Once submitted, your organization's self-certification will be reviewed by a member of the DPF team to verify that it meets the self-certification requirements. If the DPF team identifies any issues during its review of your organization's self-certification submission that must be addressed before the self-certification can be finalized, it will inform your organization via email that your organization must address all such issues within the appropriate timeframe designated by the ITA. Failure to respond within timeframes designated by the ITA or other failure to complete its self-certification in accordance with the ITA's procedures will lead to the self-certification being considered abandoned. Your organization would be informed via email once its self-certification has been finalized.

In terms of game theory, it's a Hobson's Choice—"a strategic interaction where you are presented with what at first glance seem to be multiple opportunities for free will and free choice, but where in truth you only have a single option."[26] Complying with the underlying laws and standards (i.e., GDPR) is not optional. It begs the question, is voluntarily certifying under the Privacy Shields an additional option or is it really all a single option? That's for you to ponder.

26. *See* https://www.epsilontheory.com/hobsons-choice/# (last visited Aug. 17, 2023).

# PART II

## Applying the Foundation

# CHAPTER 8

# The Role of Boards and Fiduciary Duties

As Shep Gordon states, "I think a problem for most people in a fiduciary capacity is to eliminate self and greed and all those things so that they can actually be in a fiduciary capacity where the artist comes first or the client, whoever the client happens to be."[1]

Let's begin this chapter with a reminder of two distinct but important terms—cybersecurity and cybersecurity risk management.

According to the Cybersecurity & Infrastructure Security Agency,

> Cybersecurity is the art of protecting networks, devices, and data from unauthorized access or criminal use and the practice of ensuring confidentiality, integrity, and availability of information. It seems that everything relies on computers and the internet now—communication (e.g., email, smartphones, tablets), entertainment (e.g., interactive video games, social media, apps ), transportation (e.g., navigation systems), shopping (e.g., online shopping, credit cards), medicine (e.g., medical equipment, medical records), and the list goes on.[2]

By way of contrast,

> Cyber risk management, also called cybersecurity risk management, is the process of identifying, prioritizing, managing, and monitoring risks to information systems. Companies across industries use cyber risk management to protect information systems from cyberattacks and other digital and physical threats.[3]

---

1. https://www.aarmusa.com/2021/07/28/a-key-to-rebuilding-client-agency-relationships/.

2. *What Is Cybersecurity?*, Cybersecurity & Infrastructure Security Agency (Feb. 1, 2021), https://www.cisa.gov/news-events/news/what-cybersecurity.

3. *What Is Cyber Risk Management?*, IBM, https://www.ibm.com/topics/cyber-risk-management (last visited Jan. 6, 2024).

A simplistic way to discern between "cybersecurity" and "cybersecurity risk management" is that cybersecurity focuses on the technical, administrative, and physical safeguards that are required to protect individual workstations (i.e., devices) and infrastructure to ensure that the data's confidentiality, integrity, and availability is maintained. While every person in an organization plays a role in implementing the safeguards, the onus is on the organization's chief information security officer (CISO), chief information officer (CIO), and/or an individual who coordinates with a third-party IT company (and in turn that company). Conversely, the easiest way to think of cyber risk management is through an organization's enterprise risk management plan and who has ultimate responsibility—boards and executives.

In light of the focused attacks on the healthcare industry, in late 2023, CISA released *The Mitigation Guide: Healthcare and Public Health (HPH) Sector* (hereinafter Mitigation Guide), which "provides defensive mitigation strategy recommendations and best practices to combat pervasive cyber threats affecting this critical infrastructure sector."[4] The Mitigation Guide, in an effort to assist organizations in minimizing risks pre-intrusion, also highlights known vulnerabilities.[5] Common vulnerabilities include the following:

- Web application vulnerabilities
- Encryption weaknesses
- Unsupported software
- Unsupported Windows operating systems (OS)
- Known exploited vulnerabilities (KEVs)
- Vulnerable services[6]

Hence, given the "high value of protected health information (PHI) and the criticality of patient-focused services," it should come as no surprise

4. *CISA Releases The Mitigation Guide: Healthcare and Public Health (HPH) Sector*, Cybersecurity & Infrastructure Security Agency (Nov. 17, 2023), https://www.cisa.gov/news-events/alerts/2023/11/17/cisa-releases-mitigation-guide-healthcare-and-public-health-hph-sector.

5. *Id.*

6. *See* Mitigation Guide: Healthcare and Public Health (HPH) Sector, Cybersecurity & Infrastructure Security Agency (Oct. 2023), https://www.cisa.gov/sites/default/files/2023-12/HPH-Sector-Mitigation-Guide-TLP-CLEAR._508c.pdf.

that CISA identifies asset management and security, network segmentation, identity management and device security, vulnerability, patch and configuration management, as well as evaluating risk annually through the requisite risk analysis.[7]

This notion segues into fiduciary duties and the August 4, 2023, U.S. Securities and Exchange Commission's *Cybersecurity Risk Management, Strategy, Governance, and Incident Disclosure* Final Rule.[8]

## Appreciating Fiduciary Obligations

According to Black's Law Dictionary, the term "fiduciary," which is derived from Roman law, means "a person having duty, created by his undertaking, to act primarily for another's benefit in matters connected with such undertaking. . . . A term to refer to a person having duties involving good faith, trust, special confidence, and candor towards another."[9] Typically, fiduciary duties fall into two "buckets"—the duty of loyalty and the duty of care.[10] The *Caremark and Marchand* cases[11] are essential reading in order to appreciate potential liability in terms of cybersecurity risk in relation to fiduciary duties. An excerpt from *Marchand* summarizes the *en banc* Supreme Court's position:

> Although *Caremark* may not require as much as some commentators wish, it does require that a board make a good faith effort to put in place a reasonable system of monitoring and reporting about the corporation's central compliance risks. In Blue Bell's case, food safety was essential and mission critical. The complaint pled facts supporting a fair inference that no board-level system of monitoring or reporting on food safety existed.

---

7. *Id.*

8. 88 Fed. Reg. 51896 (Aug. 4, 2023), https://www.govinfo.gov/content/pkg/FR-2023-08-04/pdf/2023-16194.pdf.

9. *See* https://blacks_law.en-academic.com/28939/fiduciary (last visited Jan. 5, 2024).

10. Tamar Frankel, 2 The New Palgrave Dictionary of Economics and the Law, Definition of "Fiduciary Duties" 127–28, https://cyber.harvard.edu/trusting/unit5all.html (last visited Jan. 5, 2024).

11. *In re Caremark Int'l Inc. Deriv. Litig.*, 698 A.2d 959, 970 (Del. Ch. 1996); *see Marchand v. Barnhill*, 212 A.3d 805 (Del. 2019).

> If *Caremark* means anything, it is that a corporate board must make a good faith effort to exercise its duty of care. A failure to make that effort constitutes a breach of duty of loyalty. Where, as here, a plaintiff has followed our admonishment to seek out relevant books and records and then uses those books and records to plead facts supporting a fair inference that no reasonable compliance system and protocols were established as to the obviously most central consumer safety and legal compliance issue facing the company, that the board's lack of efforts resulted in it not receiving official notices of food safety deficiencies for several years, and that, as a failure to take remedial action, the company exposed consumers to *listeria*-infected ice cream, resulting in the death and injury of company customers, the plaintiff has met his onerous pleading burden and is entitled to discovery to prove out his claim.[12]

Good faith forms the foundation of fiduciary duties. This notion translates directly into cybersecurity risk in relation to the duty of care to an organization, including not being educated or turning a "blind eye," and should be documented in policies and procedures, as well as in board minutes. As the rest of this chapter discusses, there are multiple considerations for not-for-profit, private, and for-profit organizations alike in the healthcare space.

## The Role of Boards and Fiduciary Duties

"Fiduciary duty requires board members to stay objective, unselfish, responsible, honest, trustworthy, and efficient."[13] Stated another way, fiduciary duties are the life force of responsible and effective governance.[14] Often times Delaware law will come into play. As it relates to cybersecurity risk management, Delaware's corporate governance principles grant

12. *Marchand*, 212 A.3d at 824.

13. *Fiduciary Responsibilities*, BoardSource, https://boardsource.org/resources/fiduciary-responsibilities/ (last updated Sept. 18, 2023).

14. *Board Fundamentals—Fiduciary Duties*, Ass'n of Governing Boards, https://agb.org/knowledge-center/board-fundamentals/fiduciary-duties/ (last visited Jan. 5, 2024).

directors with the penultimate authority to manage corporations from a cybersecurity risk standpoint.[15]

There are 6,093 hospitals in the United States, according to the American Hospital Association (AHA).[16] Of this total number, 1,228 are investor-owned (for-profit) acute care hospitals and 2,960 are nongovernment not-for-profit acute care hospitals.[17] The remainder of the 6,093 hospitals is comprised of government acute care hospitals (federal, state, or local government), psychiatric hospitals, and other hospitals.[18] All of these hospitals, regardless of their designation as for-profit, not-for-profit, or government, can likely agree on the sentiment "cybersecurity is patient safety."[19]

As of September 2022, the New York Stock Exchange (NYSE) had a combined total of 2,578 listed domestic and international companies, while the Nasdaq had 3,788, for a grand total of 6,366 publicly listed companies.[20] In March 2023, the NYSE had a combined total of 2,385 listed domestic and international companies, while the Nasdaq had 3,611—a decrease of 370 from Q3 2022.[21] The population of companies subject to the U.S. Securities and Exchange Commission (SEC) disclosure

15. Gregory A. Markel et al., *A Director's Duty of Oversight after* Marchand *in "Caremark" Case,* HARV. LAW SCH. FORUM ON CORP. GOVERNANCE (Jan. 23, 2022), https://corpgov.law.harvard.edu/2022/01/23/a-directors-duty-of-oversight-after-marchand-in-caremark-case/.

16. *Fast Facts on U.S. Hospitals, 2024,* AM. HOSP. ASS'N, https://www.aha.org/statistics/fast-facts-us-hospitals (last visited Jan. 5, 2024); Rachel V. Rose & Bob Chaput, *Why ALL Health Care Organizations Must Care about SEC Proposed Cybersecurity Rule Changes,* AHLA HEALTH LAW WEEKLY (Mar. 3, 2023), https://www.americanhealthlaw.org/content-library/health-law-weekly/article/632849de-772c-40e5-ad5c-1551ddf8d5ae/Why-ALL-Health-Care-Organizations-Must-Care-About.

17. Rose & Chaput, *supra* note 16.

18. *Id.*

19. Rachel V. Rose, *Cybersecurity Is Patient Safety,* PHYSICIANS PRACTICE (Nov. 10, 2022), https://www.physicianspractice.com/view/cybersecurity-is-patient-safety (quoting Sen. Warner's November 2022 policy paper entitled "Cybersecurity Is Patient Safety").

20. *Comparison of the Number of Listed Companies on the New York Stock Exchange (NYSE) and Nasdaq from 2018 to 3rd Quarter 2022, by Domicile,* STATISCA (Nov. 1, 2022), https://www.statista.com/statistics/1277216/nyse-nasdaq-comparison-number-listed-companies/.

21. *Comparison of the Number of Listed Companies on the New York Stock Exchange (NYSE) and Nasdaq from 2018 to 1st Quarter 2023,* by Domicile, STATISCA (May 22, 2023), https://www.statista.com/statistics/1277216/nyse-nasdaq-comparison-number-listed-companies/.

requirements is small, especially when considering the approximately 32.6 million businesses in the United States.[22] The point is that private companies dominate the U.S. economy and may not be directly subject to SEC registration, reporting, and disclosure requirements. They are, however, increasingly targeted by adversarial threat sources and subject to the same accidental, structural, and environmental threat sources that public companies face. Getting an organization's cyber risk management "ducks in a row" is not just for SEC-regulated companies.

On October 30, 2023, the SEC announced that it charged SolarWinds Corporation (SolarWinds) and its CIO with fraud and internal control failures for allegedly knowingly ignoring and misrepresenting cybersecurity risks and vulnerabilities. The complaint is illustrative of the SEC's increased focus on material misstatements and misleading reasonable investors about cybersecurity practices and known risks.[23] As alleged in its complaint,

> SolarWinds' public statements about its cybersecurity practices and risks were at odds with its internal assessments, including a 2018 presentation prepared by a company engineer and share internally, including with [CISO, Timothy T.] Brown, that SolarWinds' remote access set-up was "not very secure" and that someone exploiting the vulnerability "can basically do whatever without us detecting it until it's too late," which could lead to "major reputation and financial loss" for SolarWinds.[24]

This action underscores the notions that misrepresenting cybersecurity risks and compliance, as well as disclosing material incidents, are enforcement areas for the SEC.

---

22. *Facts & Data on Small Business and Entrepreneurship*, SMALL BUS. & ENTREPRENEURSHIP COUNCIL, https://sbecouncil.org/about-us/facts-and-data/ (last visited Jan. 5, 2024).

23. Press Release, SEC, SEC Charges SolarWinds and Chief Information Security Officer with Fraud, Internal Control Failures (Oct. 30, 2023), https://www.sec.gov/news/press-release/2023-227. On July 18, 2024, the Judge presiding over *Securities and Exchange Commission v. Solarwinds Corp. & Timothy G. Brown*, Case No. 23-cv-9518 (S.D.N.Y.) (hereinafter "*Solarwinds*") issued an Opinion and Order on Defendants' Motion to Dismiss. The pre-breach disclosure claims survived and the post-breach items were dismissed.

24. *Id.*; *see also* Securities & Exch. Comm'n v. SolarWinds Corp. & Timothy G. Brown, Case No. 1:23-cv-09518 (S.D.N.Y. Oct. 30, 2023), https://www.sec.gov/files/litigation/complaints/2023/comp-pr2023-227.pdf.

## Looking Back at the U.S. Securities and Exchange Commission's Proposed Rules and Regulations

Before delving into the SEC's August 4, 2023, *Cybersecurity Risk Management, Strategy, Governance, and Incident Disclosure* Final Rule (hereinafter Cybersecurity Final Rule),[25] it's crucial to understand what was considered in the proposed rule.

For-profit hospitals that are part of publicly traded health systems, such as Tenet Healthcare Corp. (NYSE: THC), HCA Healthcare, Inc. (NYSE: HCA), and Community Health Systems, Inc. (NYSE: CYH), have additional requirements because they are registered with the SEC and have additional obligations imposed by the related securities laws, including the Exchange Act of 1934.[26] There are also large numbers of pharmaceutical, medical device, and biotechnology companies that are publicly traded, whether as a national registrant or a foreign private issuer.[27]

On March 9, 2022, the SEC announced the release of proposed rules related to cybersecurity risk management, corporate governance, and incident disclosure by public companies.[28] Publicly traded for-profit companies (and arguably those that are registered through different avenues with the SEC) are mandated by law to comply with the proposed rules once they are finalized.[29] As Gary Gensler, SEC chair, stated, "[t]oday, cybersecurity is an emerging risk with which public issuers increasingly must contend. Investors want to know more about how issuers are

25. 88 Fed. Reg. 51896 (Aug. 4, 2023) (noting an effective date of Sept. 5, 2023).

26. *Id.*

27. *Nasdaq Healthcare & Biotech Listings*, NASDAQ, https://www.nasdaq.com/solutions/listings/markets/americas/who-can-list/industries/biotech-and-healthcare (last visited Jan. 6, 2024); *see also Medical Device and Research Stocks*, YAHOO!FINANCE, https://finance.yahoo.com/u/yahoo-finance/watchlists/medical-device-and-research-stocks/ (last visited Jan. 6, 2024).

28. 87 Fed. Reg. 16590 (Mar. 23, 2022), https://www.federalregister.gov/documents/2022/03/23/2022-05480/cybersecurity-risk-management-strategy-governance-and-incident-disclosure; Press Release, SEC, *SEC Proposes Rules on Cybersecurity Risk Management, Strategy, Governance, and Incident Disclosure by Public Companies* (Mar. 9, 2022), https://www.sec.gov/news/press-release/2022-39 (hereinafter, SEC Press Release).

29. *Fact Sheet: Public Company Cybersecurity Proposed Rules*, SEC, https://www.sec.gov/files/33-11038-fact-sheet.pdf (last visited Jan. 5, 2024).

managing those growing risks."[30] These risks also apply to non-publicly traded, not-for-profit, and government hospitals, whose executives and board members have fiduciary duties that include cybersecurity risk management.[31]

The European Union's (EU) Directive 2022/2555—Security of Network and Information Systems (NIS2) has cybersecurity mandates similar to the SEC's proposed rules; however, NIS2 extends beyond publicly traded organizations.[32] NIS2 was published and became effective on January 16, 2023, and requires cybersecurity risk management for a broad range of segments within the healthcare industry: (1) laboratories; (2) organizations engaged in research and development of medical products; and (3) medical product manufacturers, which include but are not limited to pharmaceuticals and medical devices.[33]

Like the Sarbanes-Oxley Act of 2002 (SOX),[34] in which "[s]ome hospitals have adopted SOX policies as best practices even though they are not legally bound to comply with most of its regulations,"[35] not-for-profit hospitals and health systems should consider compliance with the SEC cybersecurity rules a best practice and potentially a way to mitigate risk and be in a good position to either be acquired by a publicly traded company or fund or to go public.

This highlights how all types of healthcare organizations, as well as medical device and pharmaceutical companies and business associates,[36]

---

30. *See* SEC Press Release, *supra* note 28.

31. Jason Halper et al., *The Ramifications of The Delaware Court of Chancery's McDonald's Decision—Beyond Holding That Caremark Oversight Obligations Apply to Corporate Officers*, NAT'L LAW REV. (Feb. 9, 2023), https://www.natlawreview.com/article/ramifications-delaware-court-chancery-s-mcdonald-s-decision-beyond-holding-caremark.

32. *See* https://digital-strategy.ec.europa.eu/en/policies/nis2-directive (Jan. 16, 2023).

33. J. Giantsidis, *New EU Directive Marks Cybersecurity Regulatory Paradigm Shift for Bio/Pharma & Medical Devices*, MED DEVICE ONLINE (Feb. 15, 2023), https://www.meddeviceonline.com/doc/new-eu-directive-marks-cybersecurity-regulatory-paradigm-shift-for-bio-pharma-medical-devices-0001.

34. SOX, Pub. L. No. 107-204 (July 30, 2002).

35. Patricia Loubeau & Andrew Griffith, *Some Empirical Evidence of Sarbanes-Oxley Implementation in the Hospital Sector*, 11(1) COASTAL BUS. J. (Spring 2012), https://digitalcommons.coastal.edu/cgi/viewcontent.cgi?article=1069&context=cbj.

36. *Business Associates*, U.S. Dep't of Health & Hum. Servs., https://www.hhs.gov/hipaa/for-professionals/privacy/guidance/business-associates/index.html (last visited Feb. 11, 2023).

should consider adopting the compliance and cybersecurity risk management requirements of the SEC proposed rules, which are soon to be imposed on all publicly traded companies. The following Questions and Answers highlight key areas for organizations to consider.

## Key Questions and Suggested Considerations

### *Q1: What are the fundamental requirements of the SEC's proposed rule?*

As articulated in the text of the proposed rule, the SEC is proposing to enhance and standardize disclosures regarding cybersecurity risk management, strategy, governance, and cybersecurity incident reporting by public companies that are subject to the reporting requirements of the Securities Exchange Act of 1934. Specifically, we are proposing amendments to require current reporting about material cybersecurity incidents. We are also proposing to require periodic disclosures about a registrant's policies and procedures to identify and manage cybersecurity risks, management's role in implementing cybersecurity policies and procedures, and the board of directors' cybersecurity expertise, if any, and its oversight of cybersecurity risk.[37]

Disclosure of cybersecurity incidents are material in SEC filings and to the public. Under the Health Insurance Portability and Accountability Act of 1996 (HIPAA) Breach Notification Rule,[38] as well as the Federal Trade Commission's Health Breach Notification Rule,[39] there are additional disclosure requirements for HIPAA covered entities, business associates, and subcontractors, as well as persons who handle personal health records.[40]

37. 87 Fed. Reg. 16590.

38. 45 C.F.R. § 164.400–.414.

39. Rachel V. Rose, *Cybersecurity Risk Considerations after the FTC's First Breach Notification Settlement*, Physicians Practice (Feb. 9, 2023), https://www.physicianspractice.com/view/cybersecurity-risk-considerations-after-the-ftc-s-first-breach-notification-settlement.

40. *Id.*

## Q2: Why are these changes being proposed?

Cybersecurity risks and incidents can impact the financial performance or position of a company. Consistent, comparable, and decision-useful disclosures regarding an organization's cybersecurity risk management, strategy, and governance practices, as well as a company's response to material cybersecurity incidents, would allow investors to understand such risks and incidents, evaluate a company's risk management and governance practices regarding those risks, and better inform their investment and voting decisions.[41] In recent testimony before the U.S. Senate Committee on Banking, Housing, and Urban Affairs, as it relates to public company disclosures, SEC Chairman Gary Gensler, stated, "For the last 90 years, our capital markets have relied on a basic bargain. Investors get to decide which risks to take as long as companies provide full, fair, and truthful disclosures. Congress tasked the SEC with overseeing this bargain. We do so through a disclosure-based regime, not a merit-based one."[42] The proposed cybersecurity disclosure rule changes are all about what the SEC believes are full, fair, and truthful disclosures. "The proposed amendments are intended to better inform investors about a registrant's risk management, strategy, and governance and to provide timely notification of material cybersecurity incidents."[43]

## Q3: When could these proposed changes be implemented?

The Notice of Proposed Rule Making was published in the *Federal Register* on March 23, 2022, and comments were initially due by May 9, 2022. The comment period was extended, with a total of 156 comments submitted as of this writing.[44] Although there is always the possibility of delays in rulemaking, the SEC's timetable for these changes shows final

---

41. Bob Chaput, *Overview of the SEC "Cybersecurity Risk Management, Strategy, Governance, and Incident Disclosure" Proposed Rule Changes*, https://clearwatercompliance.com/blog/overview-of-the-sec-cybersecurity-risk-management-strategy-governance-and-incident-disclosure-proposed-rule-changes/ (last visited Jan. 5, 2024).

42. Gary Gensler, *Testimony before the United States Senate Committee on Banking, Housing, and Urban Affairs*, SEC (Sept. 15, 2022), https://www.sec.gov/news/testimony/gensler-testimony-housing-urban-affairs-091522.

43. 87 Fed. Reg. 16590.

44. *Comments on the Cybersecurity Risk Management, Strategy, Governance, and Incident Disclosure*, SEC, https://www.sec.gov/comments/s7-09-22/s70922.htm (last visited Jan. 5, 2024).

action by April 2023.[45] This anticipated timeframe was not met, as the Final Rule was published on August 4, 2023 in the *Federal Register*.

## *Q4: Why should private and not-for-profit organizations also adhere to the SEC's proposed rule?*

1. **The SEC has the authority to investigate all companies that seek to raise capital from U.S. investors.** Among other avenues, investors in private companies often exit by way of an initial public offering and going public. SEC's oversight includes all public and private companies making any false or misleading statements as part of an offering process.
2. **A strategic acquirer of a private company may already be public and currently subject to SEC disclosure requirements.** In this case, any potential acquirer would already be filing required cyber-related reports and disclosures and would place value on any private company efforts to not only easily make the disclosures but, more importantly, to have a mature enterprise cyber-risk management program in place. According to a recent *Forescout* report, 48 percent of business leaders encountered a critical cyber issue or incident during an M&A transaction that jeopardized the deal.[46]
3. **Protect current stakeholders.** Private companies and not-for-profit organizations have customers, perhaps patients, investors, bankers, insurers, employees, and regulators (think: HIPAA, Gramm-Leach-Bliley Act, Family Educational Rights and Privacy Act, General Data Protection Regulation, etc.), all of whom expect the organization to have and benefit from a robust cyber-risk management.
4. **The cost of capital is lower for all organizations that establish, implement, and mature an enterprise cyber-risk management program.** Credit-rating agencies—including Standard and Poor's, Moody's, and Fitch Group—have all implemented consideration

45. *Cyber Risk Governance,* SEC (Spring 2022), https://www.reginfo.gov/public/do/eAgendaViewRule?pubId=202204&RIN=3235-AM89.

46. *The Role of Cybersecurity in M&A Diligence,* Forescout (2019), https://www.forescout.com/merger-and-acquisition-cybersecurity-report/.

of the financial impact of a cyberattack on an organization's credit rating. Moody's downgraded the credit rating for Equifax from "stable" to "negative" based on the immense data breach the company experienced in 2017.[47]

5. **Most private companies are part of public company supply chains.** Heads up, even though you may serve on the board of a private company, your customers and vendors may be public companies. When the proposed SEC cyber-disclosure requirements are finalized, expect to have your public company stakeholders raise the ante in terms of your incident response and reporting to them. We saw similar requirements tighten when the Omnibus Final Rule codifying the Health Information Technology for Economic and Clinical Health Act was published in the *Federal Register* in 2013.[48]
6. **Manage talent risk in the new world.** COVID-19, the "Great Resignation," big tech layoffs, and "quiet quitting" have created a new set of dynamics for organizations striving to attract and retain talent for their organizations. Organizations with tainted reputations due to material cyber incidents will likely have a more difficult time with talent management, now a board issue. Specific to cybersecurity talent, how competitive will your company be in attracting cybersecurity professionals in the face of the current shortage of 3.4 million cybersecurity workers worldwide?[49]

Whether addressing HIPAA or the SEC's proposal, companies should already have committed to cultivating a culture of compliance by continually addressing technical, administrative, and physical safeguards, approaching cybersecurity from the vantage points of prevention,

---

47. Nicole Lindsey, *Equifax Downgrade Shows the Lasting Financial Impact of a Massive Data Breach*, CPO MAG. (June 3, 2019), https://www.cpomagazine.com/cyber-security/equifax-downgrade-shows-the-lasting-financial-impact-of-a-massive-data-breach/.

48. *Business Associate Contracts*, U.S. DEP'T OF HEALTH & HUM. SERVS., https://www.hhs.gov/hipaa/for-professionals/covered-entities/sample-business-associate-agreement-provisions/index.html (last visited Jan. 5, 2024); *see also* 78 Fed. Reg. 5566 (Jan. 25, 2013).

49. ISC2, *(ISC)2 CYBERSECURITY WORKFORCE STUDY 2022* (Oct. 17, 2022), https://www.isc2.org/-/media/Project/ISC2/Main/Media/documents/research/ISC2-Cybersecurity-Workforce-Study.pdf?rev=ae39d66a4616478792d38da57fb80564&hash=31B8381DC81AD70B9B6DA6FF84534B33.

detection, and correction. It is imperative for public, private, and not-for-profit healthcare organizations alike to ensure that adequate documentation exists to substantiate ongoing compliance because the public market, insurance companies, and banks issuing lines of credit will all require cybersecurity risk management.

## The SEC's Final Rule a Focus on Reasonableness and Materiality in Relation to Prevention, Detection, and Correction

The word "material" appears 355 times in the Cybersecurity Final Rule. That fact alone should cause counsel, compliance leaders, executives, and board members alike, as well as their auditors and the organization itself, to sit up and take note. The Cybersecurity Final Rule has four main areas of focus.

> Specifically, we are adopting amendments to require current disclosure about material cybersecurity incidents. We are also adopting rules requiring periodic disclosures about a registrant's processes to assess, identify, and manage material cybersecurity risks, management's role in assessing and managing material cybersecurity risks, and the board of directors' oversight of cybersecurity risks. Lastly, the final rules require the cybersecurity disclosures to be presented in Inline eXtensible Business Reporting Language ("Inline XBRL").[50]

These requirements apply to both national registrants and foreign private issuers (FPIs) and build upon prior guidance. For example, the 2011 Staff Guidance provides that "[a]lthough no existing disclosure requirement explicitly refers to cybersecurity risks and cyber incidents, a number of disclosure requirements may impose an obligation on registrants to disclose such risks and incidents," and further that "material information regarding cybersecurity risks and cyber incidents is required to be disclosed when necessary in order to make other required disclosures, in light of the circumstances under which they are made, not misleading."

---

50. 88 Fed. Reg. at 51896.

Indeed, material cybersecurity risks and disclosures are not new. Companies, including healthcare companies such as Community Health Systems[51] and Tenet Healthcare,[52] have disclosed material cybersecurity items in their respective SEC filings for at least a decade. This raises a related issue—what if HIPAA and GDPR have different reporting requirements? The SEC addresses this issue, primarily at 88 Fed. Reg. 51297.

> HIPAA requires covered entities and their business associates to provide notification following a breach of unsecured protected health information. Similar rules require vendors of personal health records and related entities to report data breaches to affected individuals and the FTC. All 50 states have data breach laws that require businesses to notify individuals of security breaches involving their personally identifiable information. There are other rules that registrants must follow in international jurisdictions. For example, in the European Union, the General Data Protection Regulation mandates disclosure of cybersecurity breaches (internal citations omitted).
>
> ...
>
> Under HIPAA regulations, covered entities are subject to rules that require protection against reasonably anticipated threats to electronic protected health information. International jurisdictions also have cybersecurity risk mitigation measures and governance requirements (see, for example, the GDPR). These rules and regulations provide varying standards and requirements for disclosing cybersecurity risk management, strategy, and governance, and may not provide investors with public or clear and comparable disclosure regarding how a particular registrant manages its cybersecurity risk profile (internal citations omitted).

---

51. *Form 8-K,* Community Health Systems (Aug. 18, 2014), https://www.sec.gov/Archives/edgar/data/1108109/000119312514312504/d776541d8k.htm ("confirm[ing] that its computer network was the target of an external, criminal cyber attack that the Company believes occurred in April and June, 2014").

52. *Tenet Healthcare Cyberattack Cost $100 Million,* Security Mag. (Aug. 1, 2022), https://www.securitymagazine.com/articles/98089-tenet-healthcare-cyberattack-cost-100-million.

Overall, in healthcare, covered entities and business associates alike who fall under the SEC's jurisdiction must meet the requirements of each law. Likewise, if a company, an FPI for example, is required to meet international legal obligations, such as GDPR, then those companies need to meet that requirement and the SEC disclosure requirements.

This brings us back to the key terms—material and reasonable. As discussed in a *Bloomberg Law* article co-authored by one of this book's authors, [a] close look at these terms—and how the SEC and courts have interpreted them—will be a useful guide to those affected by the new rule.

## Materiality

The "material" impact of a cyber incident on a registrant is central to the determination of whether to notify the SEC with a Form 8-K, and in turn the market and investors.

Materiality is a core consideration in determining whether any risk from cybersecurity threats, including as a result of any previous cybersecurity incidents, exists. Legal counsel, cybersecurity consultants, and the registrants should utilize industry standards such as the National Institute of Standards and Technology and other laws such as HIPAA or GDPR to ascertain whether an event or lack of safeguards is material.

If a disclosure is required, they should accurately state the facts and circumstances in SEC filings and in any other public disclosures, such as on the company's website.

Incidents that have affected or are reasonably likely to affect an organization, including its business strategy, results of operations, or financial condition are considered material.[53] This could lead to potential violations under SEC Rule 17(a) or Rule 10(b)-5, which relate to material commissions and omissions in relation to disclosures.

The U.S. Supreme Court has provided a roadmap in its cases addressing materiality in securities laws, including TSC Industries, Inc. v. Northway, Inc., Basic, Inc. v. Levinson, and Matrixx Initiatives, Inc. v.

53. Rachel V. Rose, Andy Watkin-Child, Ted Dziekanowski, *SEC Cybersecurity Rule Leans on Materiality and Reasonableness*, Bloomberg Law (Aug. 18, 2023), https://news.bloomberglaw.com/us-law-week/sec-cybersecurity-rule-leans-on-materiality-and-reasonableness.

Siracusano,[54] coupled with the SEC's rules, 17 C.F.R. § 230.405 and 17 C.F.R. § 240.12b-2.

The law, whether affirmed by the Supreme Court or maintained in regulations, indicates that information "is material if there is a 'substantial likelihood that a reasonable shareholder would consider it important' in making an investment decision, or if it would have significantly altered the 'total mix' of information made available."[55]

## Reasonable Investor

This leads to the "reasonable investor," which can be compared to the legal definition of a "reasonable person." A "reasonable person" is a "hypothetical person who exercises qualities of attention, knowledge, intelligence, and judgment that society requires of its members for the protection of their own interest and the interests of others."[56] This concept is not new. The renowned 1837 English court of common pleas case, *Vaughn v. Menlove,*[57] established that, in the common law, the reasonable person standard is that of "a man of ordinary prudence" thereby making the standard objective. This common law standard has been used as the basis of both state and federal common law in the United States. In a securities law case, the Supreme Court in *Omnicare Inc. v. Laborers District Council Construction Industry Pension Fund,*[58] held that the inquiry into whether an omission of a material fact makes a statement misleading must be viewed from the reasonable investor's perspective, much like the determination of materiality.

---

54. TSC Industries, Inc. v. Northway, Inc., 426 U.S. 438 (1976); Basic, Inc. v. Levinson, 485 U.S. 224 (1988); and Matrixx Initiatives, Inc. v. Siracusano, 563 U.S. 27 (2011).

55. The standard of materiality articulated by the U.S. Supreme Court in TSC Industries v. Northway, 426 U.S. 438, 449 (1976) (a fact is material "if there is a substantial likelihood that a reasonable shareholder would consider it important" in making an investment decision or if it "would have been viewed by the reasonable investor as having significantly altered the 'total mix' of information made available" to the shareholder).

56. https://www.trans-lex.org/124800/_/joachim-willi-e-the-reasonable-man-in-united-states-and-german-commercial-law-15-complybint-l-bus-1992-at-341-et-seq/

57. Vaughn v. Menlove, 132 Eng. Rep. 490 (1837).

58. Omnicare Inc. v. Laborers Dist. Council Constr. Indus. Pension Fund, 125 S. Ct. 1318 (2015).

Companies required to make disclosures and disclose their cybersecurity risk management and governance must consider what is material to a reasonable investor.

This increases the level of language granularity and simplicity that persons should utilize, as the materiality bar is lower for the reasonable investor than for sophisticated or institutional market investors.

Importantly, what is disclosed must be balanced with providing too much information, which in turn could make the entity more vulnerable to an attack or other form of exploitation.

Overall, appreciating that cybersecurity is now more important than ever to reasonable investors because of the costs—financial, reputational, and legal—should encourage executives, workforce members, and boards of directors to evaluate risk and the vital role everyone plays in ensuring that technical, administrative, and physical safeguards are implemented and adhered to.

## The Cost of Ignoring Cybersecurity Risks for the Board, the Executives, and the Company

Most people have heard the adage "orange is not my color." This refers to the notion that the orange jumpsuits worn by prisoners are not flattering in either color, form, or what they signify. Placed into a fiduciary context, boards, along with executives and IT professionals, should always think of potential criminal implications first and foremost. For example, HIPAA and select countries that fall under the EU's GDPR umbrella, can expose individuals and corporations to criminal liability.[59] On April 25, 2023, the DOJ announced that multiple former hospital employees who co-conspired with an outsider to steal PHI and sell it for remuneration to third parties, including personal injury attorneys and chiropractors,

59. *See* https://gdpr-info.eu/issues/fines-penalties/ (last visited Jan. 5, 2024); *see also* 42 U.S.C. § 1320d-6 (indicating that violating HIPAA can result in criminal penalties "if the offense is committed with intent to sell, transfer, or use individually identifiable health information for commercial advantage, personal gain, or malicious harm, be fined not more than $250,000, imprisoned not more than 10 years, or both").

entered guilty pleas.[60] Sentencing was scheduled for later in the summer of 2023 and, ultimately, in February 2024, one of the defendants, Roderick Harvey, was sentenced to five years of probation, one of which was to be served in his home, and a $50,000 fine.[61]

This type of potential liability should not come as a surprise, especially because the DOJ has international reach and HIPAA itself added 18 U.S.C. § 3486, which "empowers the Attorney General, or the Attorney General's designee, to issue investigative demands to obtain records for investigations relating to Federal criminal health care fraud offense."[62] When seeking discovery abroad, the following sources should be consulted: the Federal Rules of Civil Procedure, the Hague Convention, letters rogatory (i.e., formal request from a U.S. judge when an action is pending in a foreign court asking for assistance in the performance of a judicial act); the Walsh Act (28 U.S.C. § 1783) (authorizing a federal court to issue a subpoena for documents or testimony from a U.S. citizen or resident abroad under certain circumstances in both civil and criminal proceedings); and utilizing a foreign jurisdiction's process.[63]

It's important to consider breach of fiduciary duty from both a U.S. and another country's vantage point. In the United States, as the DOJ summarizes in its Criminal Resource Manual,

> At the core of the judicially defined "scheme to defraud" is the notion of a trust owed to another and a subsequent breach of that trust. *United States v. Lemire,* 720 F.2d 1327, 1335 (D.C. Cir. 1983) ('But '[n]ot every breach of a fiduciary duty works a criminal fraud.') (quoting *United States v. George,* 477 F.2d 508

---

60. Press Release, DOJ, Former Methodist Hospital Employees Plead Guilty to HIPAA Violations (Apr. 25, 2023), https://www.justice.gov/usao-wdtn/pr/former-methodist-hospital-employees-plead-guilty-hipaa-violations; *see also* https://www.campussafetymagazine.com/news/5-former-tennessee-hospital-employees-charged-with-hipaa-violations/ (Feb. 6, 2024).

61. *Id.*

62. *Justice Manual -9-44.000 Health Care Fraud,* U.S. Dep't of Just., https://www.justice.gov/jm/jm-9-44000-health-care-fraud (last visited Jan. 5, 2024).

63. Aimée Canty, *Getting Discovery Across Borders—Four Tips (and Some Obstacles) for Litigation across International Lines* (Am. Bar Ass'n Mar. 23, 2020), https://www.americanbar.org/groups/litigation/committees/pretrial-practice-discovery/practice/2020/getting-discovery-across-borders/.

> (7th Cir.), *cert. denied,* 414 U.S. 827 (1973)), *cert. denied,* 467 U.S. 1226 (1984). *But cf. United States v. Sawyer,* 878 F. Supp. 279, 288-90 (D. Mass. 1995) (mail fraud statutes do not require that a public fiduciary be a participant in the scheme). It may follow that to defraud one of the "right to honest services" would generally require a fiduciary relationship that creates the right to provide or protect honest services. It does not necessarily follow, however, that the existence or protection of an intangible property right must depend upon the existence of a fiduciary relationship or duty. Nonfiduciaries can steal, embezzle and defraud others of property interests, regardless of whether the property interest is tangible or intangible. *Cf. United States v. Allen,* 554 F.2d 398, 410 (10th Cir.) ('While the existence of a fiduciary duty is relevant and an ingredient in some mail fraud prosecutions, . . . it is not an essential in all such cases.') (citations omitted), *cert. denied,* 434 U.S. 836 (1977); Eilers & Silikovitz, 31 Am. Crim. L. Rev. at 711 ('There is some debate in the Circuit Courts about whether intangible rights can be violated if they are not premised upon fiduciary duty.').[64]

By way of contrast, in Austria, "[o]ne of the most discussed provisions of Austrian business criminal law is breach of fiduciary duty (Untreue) under Art 153 StGB (Strafgesetzbuch—Austrian Criminal Code, StGB)."[65] Tying the breach of fiduciary duty back to potential liability for not being both educated and involved in monitoring cybersecurity risk—civil is the usual course of action that private persons and governmental entities will pursue. Importantly, a governmental entity, whether local, state, or federal, may pursue a criminal action on the U.S. side. On the international front, if a criminal action ensues, that country's law enforcement arm may coordinate with the United States.

---

64. *CRM 947—Fiduciary Duty,* U.S. Dep't of Just., https://www.justice.gov/archives/jm/criminal-resource-manual-947-fiduciary-duty (last visited Jan. 5, 2024).

65. Wolf Theiss, *Criminal Law: Breach of Fiduciary Duty: Can a Principal Effectively Consent to Actions of His or Her Representative and Thus Exclude Criminal Liability?,* Lexology (Feb. 12, 2019), https://www.lexology.com/library/detail.aspx?g=12efe90b-a4ae-4ab0-967e-bb63f48d7755.

As in every area of law, it comes down to individual facts and circumstances. Appreciating that this potential liability exists should be incorporated into board-level discussions, as well as into an organization's compliance training and enterprise risk management strategy. Given the SEC's focus on both national registrants and FPIs, cybersecurity compliance cannot be overlooked by companies located in the United States, and abroad, that are traded on the U.S. exchanges (i.e., NYSE and Nasdaq) and are included in different indexes (i.e., S&P 500, the Dow, and the Nasdaq Composite).[66]

66. Chizoba Morah, *What Are All of the Major US Stock Exchanges?*, Investopedia (updated May 15, 2022), https://www.investopedia.com/ask/answers/08/security-market-usa.asp; *see also* Rakesh Sharma, *Nasdaq Composite vs. S&P 500 vs. Dow: What's the Difference?*, https://www.investopedia.com/nasdaq-vs-sp500-vs-dow-5213252#:~:text=The%20S%26P%20500%2C%20the%20Dow,move%20in%20the%20same%20direction (last updated Mar. 17, 2024).

# PART III

# Conclusion

Cyberattacks on healthcare providers and lawyers alike are on the increase because of the sensitive and profitable data they possess.[1] Because law firms may be considered business associates or subcontractors under HIPAA or processors under NGDPR, and hospitals and other providers are covered entities under HIPAA, assessing cybersecurity risk on at least an annual basis is critical.[2]

---

1. *Levales Solicitors Data Breach on April 14, 2023*, BREACHSENSE, https://www.breachsense.io/breaches/levales-solicitors-data-breach/ (last visited Apr. 16, 2023); Apurva Venkat, *Bian Lian Ransomware Group Shifts Focus to Extortion*, CSO, (Mar. 20, 2023), https://www.csoonline.com/article/3691130/bianlian-ransomware-group-shifts-focus-to-extortion.html (indicating that BianLian, a known ransomware group, shifted its focus away from encrypting files and toward extortion in order to realize monetary gains); *see also* Sara Merken, *N.Y. Law Firm to Pay State $200K over Data Breach*, REUTERS (Mar. 27, 2023), https://www.reuters.com/legal/litigation/ny-law-firm-pay-state-200k-over-data-breach-2023-03-27/ (relaying that the New York attorney general agreed to a $200,000 settlement with a mid-size law firm over a 2021 data breach that occurred as a result of data security lapses).

2. Alexis Zacharakos, *No Relief in Sight for Ransomware Attacks on Hospitals*, TECHTARGET (Feb. 16, 2023), https://www.techtarget.com/searchsecurity/feature/No-relief-in-sight-for-ransomware-attacks-on-hospitals (referencing a Sophos report, "the threat detection vendor found that 66% of the 381 healthcare organizations involved in the study were victim to ransomware attacks that year—an increase of about 50% from 2021").

# CHAPTER 9

# Practical Compliance Suggestions

As Henry David Thoreau stated in *Walden*, "[i]f you have built castles in the air, your work need not be lost; that is where they should be. Now put the foundations under them." The main take-away from Thoreau, as it relates to cybersecurity compliance and risk management programs is that although an established person should have implemented adequate technical, administrative, and physical safeguards long before now, putting in a new foundation now is better than having the company collapse. Covered entities and business associates such as law firms have been the subject of court decisions, including a unanimous September 2, 2022, U.S. Court of Appeals for the Third Circuit opinion, whereby "class-action suits over data breaches no longer require proof of actual harm."[1] This underscores the importance of post-incident correction and annual prevention, which includes revisions to an organization's compliance program and cyber risk management.

## Post-Incident Correction and Annual Prevention

A great place to begin is with the seven core items required of any compliance program. As set forth in 42 C.F.R. § 422.503(b)(4)(iv), the items are as follows:

1. Training and education
2. Written policies and procedures, as well as standards of conduct
3. Effective lines of communication—both between an organization's employees and partnering entities
4. Known disciplinary standards (i.e., exclusion from federal programs, tiered sanctions policies for HIPAA violations)

1. Jennifer Clemens v. Execupharm Inc.; Parexel Int'l Corp., Case No. 21-506 (3d Cir. Sept. 2, 2022), https://www2.ca3.uscourts.gov/opinarch/211506p.pdf.

5. Effective system for routine monitoring and compliance risk identification
6. Procedures and system for prompt response to compliance issues
7. Designation of a Compliance Officer

Next, assess a current HIPAA compliance program or a new HIPAA compliance program from a prevention, detection, and correction vantage point utilizing the HIPAA Security Rule, 405(d) resources, which were compiled as part of a public-private initiative as mandated by the Cybersecurity Act of 2015, NIST and FIPS publications, and the Cybersecurity and Infrastructure Security Agency's (CISA's) *High-Level Zero Trust Maturity Model Overview*[2] (see Figure 4.1 on page 34).

Finally, ensure that a knowledgeable third-party conduct an annual risk analysis in an impartial manner and that identified "gaps" are corrected.

## The Role of Insurance

Cyber insurance should be a cornerstone of cyber risk management. As a recent *Forbes* article relayed, "[a]ccording to Cybersecurity Ventures, by 2025, it is predicted that the world will suffer a loss of $10.5 trillion yearly due to cybercrime. This estimate underscores the catastrophic implications of cybercrime, which has been identified as the greatest transfer of economic wealth in history."[3] As an insurer espouses, persons seeking professional liability and cyber insurance are exposed to the deficiencies in definitions leading to silent cyber questions.[4]

Insurance companies, including Lloyd's of London, are requiring an application for cyber insurance to reduce the following: unnecessary

---

2. *See* https://www.cisa.gov/zero-trust-maturity-model (last visited Apr. 15, 2023); https://405d.hhs.gov (last visited Apr. 15, 2023); *Addressing Gaps in Cybersecurity: OCR Releases Crosswalk between HIPAA Security Rule and NIST Cybersecurity Framework*, U.S. Dep't of Health & Hum. Servs., https://www.hhs.gov/hipaa/for-professionals/security/nist-security-hipaa-crosswalk/index.html (last visited Apr. 15, 2023).

3. Tracy Levine, *Don't Leave Your Law Practice Vulnerable: The Legal Obligation to Protect against Cyberattacks*, Forbes (Mar. 14, 2023), https://www.forbes.com/sites/forbestechcouncil/2023/03/14/dont-leave-your-law-practice-vulnerable-the-legal-obligation-to-protect-against-cyberattacks/?sh=a6be65032a29.

4. *See* https://www.marsh.com/uk/services/cyber-risk/products/silent-cyber-how-you-can-cover-perils.html (last visited Apr. 15, 2023).

premium expenditure; coverage disputes between carriers; elevated post-loss costs; and delays in claim settlement.[5] This practice builds upon industry observations about the most common reasons that claims are rejected.[6] Adequate documentation and inadequate cyber hygiene are fundamental reasons why insurance claims related to cybersecurity incidents get rejected.[7] In other words, ensuring that technical, administrative, and physical safeguards are in place is critical to both receiving approval for cyber insurance and for demonstrating continued compliance efforts in the event of a claim for coverage.

## Obtaining Reasonable Assurances

As set forth by HHS, "The Privacy Rule allows covered providers and health plans to disclose protected health information to these "business associates" if the providers or plans obtain satisfactory assurances that the business associate will use the information only for the purposes for which it was engaged by the covered entity, will safeguard the information from misuse, and will help the covered entity comply with some of the covered entity's duties under the Privacy Rule."[8] This requirement is often set forth in the BAA; however, prior to signing a BAA, it is prudent to have a five-question attestation executed.

As Roger Severino, former director of HHS-Office of Civil Rights stated, "[f]or enforcement purposes, there's still a lot of low-hanging fruit. . . . [t]here are a lot of entities that are not doing the basic steps to make sure they have proper, for example, cybersecurity protections in place. They're not doing a comprehensive risk analyses on the front end."[9] Therefore, by asking a party to a BAA to attest to these five

---

5. *Id.*

6. *See* https://blog.ariacybersecurity.com/blog/machine-learning-ai-in-cybersecurity-solutions (Feb. 7, 2022).

7. Cyber Management Alliance, *Why Do Cyber Insurance Claims Get Rejected?* (Sept. 21, 2023), https://www.cm-alliance.com/cybersecurity-blog/why-do-cyber-insurance-claims-get-rejected.

8. *Business Associates,* U.S. Dep't of Health & Hum. Servs., https://www.hhs.gov/hipaa/for-professionals/privacy/guidance/business-associates/index.html (last visited Apr. 15, 2023).

9. Jeff Overly, *HIPAA Boss Sees "Low-Hanging Fruit" Ripe for Enforcement,* Law360 (Feb. 3, 2020), https://www.law360.com/articles/1233269/hipaa-boss-sees-low-hanging-fruit-ripe-for-enforcement.

questions, one can quickly discern whether or not there is adequate compliance and if they want to take a risk in doing business with this person. The five suggested questions are as follows:

1. Is an annual risk analysis conducted?
2. Is training done and documented at least annually?
3. Are there comprehensive policies and procedures?
4. Is data encrypted both at rest and in transit?
5. Are BAA in place when appropriate and have the entities provided reasonable assurances?

Another area to consider is "data poaching." Two recent FTC cases brought this to light. Specifically, two recent enforcement action settlements, which occurred between February and early March 2023, underscore its authority and both are notable for distinct reasons:

- **GoodRx (February 1, 2023).** GoodRX is the first case where an enforcement action was taken under the FTC's Health Breach Notification Rule. Here, GoodRx, a telehealth and prescription drug discount provider "fail[ed] to notify consumers and other of its unauthorized disclosures of consumers' personal health information to Facebook, Google, and other companies." Moreover, "[i]n a first-of-its-kind proposed order, filed by the Department of Justice on behalf of the FTC, GoodRx will be prohibited from sharing user health data with applicable third parties for advertising purposes, and has agreed to pay a $1.5 million civil penalty for violating the rule. The proposed order must be approved by the federal court to go into effect." GoodRx paid the government $7.8 million to settle the allegations.[10]
- **BetterHelp, Inc. (March 2, 2023).** In another first-of-its-kind case, the FTC provided remuneration to customer who were harmed by "online counseling service BetterHelp revealed

10. *See* Press Release, FTC, FTC Enforcement Action to Bar GoodRx from Sharing Consumers' Sensitive Health Info for Advertising (Feb. 1, 2023), https://www.ftc.gov/news-events/news/press-releases/2023/02/ftc-enforcement-action-bar-goodrx-sharing-consumers-sensitive-health-info-advertising.

consumers' sensitive data with third parties such as Facebook and Snapchat for advertising after promising to keep such data private."[11]

A separate attestation addressing this should be done whenever a new person is being considered as a BAA party and during each annual risk analysis, as the subcontractors could have changed. The four questions are as follows:

| |
|---|
| 1. Do you promise users that you won't share personal health information with advertisers or other third parties? |
| 2. If you do share information with Facebook, Google, Yelp, etc., or other third parties, do you obtain patient consent? |
| 3. Do you conduct adequate due diligence on your third parties, including business associates, to ensure that they have adequate safeguards in place? |
| 4. Do you or your third-party vendors misrepresent HIPAA compliance, including monetizing PHI for advertising purposes? |

## Business Associate Agreements in the International Arena

Fortunately, from a contractual standpoint, not much has changed from what we published in Chapters 4 and 5 in *What Are International HIPAA Considerations?* In addition to what is presented in this chapter, parties should also consider the following:

| |
|---|
| 1. Data poaching by third parties |
| 2. Assurances of cyber liability insurance |
| 3. Biometric laws |
| 4. Reproductive health-related PHI |
| 5. Individual country laws |

11. *See* Press Release, FTC, FTC to Ban BetterHelp from Revealing Consumers' Data, including Sensitive Mental Health Information, to Facebook and Others for Targeted Advertising (Mar. 2, 2023), https://www.ftc.gov/news-events/news/press-releases/2023/03/ftc-ban-betterhelp-revealing-consumers-data-including-sensitive-mental-health-information-facebook.

## Contractual Considerations and Jurisdiction over Breaches/Civil Liability of Overseas Business Associates

> "Our foreign subsidiaries hold 70 percent of our cash because of the very rapid growth of our international business. We use these earnings to fund our foreign operations, such as spending billions of dollars to acquire equipment to make Apple products and to finance construction of Apple retail stores around the world."
>
> —Tim Cook, CEO, Apple

As Apple's CEO, Tim Cook indicated a lot of growth is occurring in international markets. And, this is not limited to Apple products. This is a key consideration for practitioners and businesses alike. Microsoft stated, "[t]he internet and cloud computing are erasing geographic boundaries for the flow of information. The Internet makes it possible for a business in one country to run a website or store data in a second country, and conduct transactions with customers the world over."[12] Some key points that can mitigate legal, reputational, and financial risk in relation to cloud computing include the following:

- Cloud computing and international commerce are limited by conflicting international laws and regulations governing the privacy of data sent across national borders.
- Microsoft supports efforts to develop globally consistent policy frameworks that recognize the worldwide nature of data exchanges while providing strong privacy protection. Governments need to help develop clear rules and regulations that resolve conflicting privacy obligations.
- International privacy standards should be flexible, applied across industry sectors, and technology neutral. Strong collaboration among industry, government, and civil society is needed to achieve the right balance.[13]

---

12. https://www.microsoft.com/en-us/trust-center/privacy.

13. *Id.* While not meant to be a "commercial" for Microsoft, having reviewed many company policies and position papers, their company, along with Apple, IngramMicro, and

In October 2010, The 32nd International Conference of Data Protection and Privacy Commissioners adopted a resolution—*Resolution on Privacy by Design.*[14] The concepts espoused are general, but important, and coincide with Microsoft's goals. In particular and related to HIPAA and corollary laws in other countries, privacy needs to be embedded across all channels and throughout the information's life cycle.[15] As such, it is prudent to have accessible a team of lawyers who are well versed in healthcare laws and international laws and procedures.

## *Does DHHS Have Explicit Overseas Enforcement Authority over the CE, BA, and Subcontractor?*

Yes. There is nothing precluding the reach of the attorney general to enforce HIPAA violations overseas. While additional laws such as Japan's Act on the Protection of Personal Information[16] may apply, express authorization by section 248 of HIPAA enables the attorney general to issue

---

Cisco are among the leaders. Not only do they write policies and procedures, they are the most likely to adhere to them. And, Microsoft's Approach, serves as a good guideline.

"Microsoft's longstanding commitment to privacy includes principles, policies, and procedures for building privacy protections into its products and services, from development through deployment and operation.

- Microsoft's privacy standards govern the development and deployment of Microsoft products and services. These standards, a version of which have been made public, offer detailed guidance on customer notification and consent procedures, help make sure data security features are sufficient, maintain data integrity, and provide user access and controls. Microsoft also helps to protect customers by delivering more secure products through the Microsoft Security Development Lifecycle ("SDL"), a software security assurance process which embeds security and privacy throughout product development. Microsoft designs its cloud services to help ensure data security and user privacy.
- Microsoft works to help ensure that employees, vendors, and partners are accountable for the handling of customers' personal information. Each Microsoft business unit is responsible for developing procedures to strengthen and support accountability, and for assigning specific staff members the day-to-day responsibilities of monitoring and protecting privacy.

Microsoft follows and implements international privacy and data protection standards."

14. 32nd International Conference of Data Protection and Privacy Commissioners (Oct. 2010), https://secure.edps.europa.eu/EDPSWEB/webdav/site/mySite/shared/Documents/Cooperation/Conference_int/10-10-27_Jerusalem_Resolutionon_PrivacybyDesign_EN.pdf.

15. *Id.*

16. Act No. 57 of 2003 (APPI). This law and relevant guidelines apply to personal information, personal data and personal information databases.

subpoenas and request the production of certain documents, testimony, and other relevant information in relation to "any act or activity involving a federal health care offense."[17] Production can be compelled for "(1) any records or other things relevant to the investigation and (2) testimony by the custodian of the things required to be produced concerning the production and authenticity of those things."[18] In relation to HIPAA, a subpoena could be issued to a business associate who reviews records in India, and all items related to the investigation into the potential violations of U.S. healthcare laws can be requested for production.

This is in keeping with the U.S. Department of Justice's (DOJ's) report to Congress.

> In evaluating the scope of an administrative subpoena issued under 18 U.S.C. § 3486(a)(1)(A)(i)(I), the federal courts apply the principle formulated by the Supreme Court in *Oklahoma Press*, generally applicable to executive branch administrative subpoenas, that an administrative subpoena must be "reasonably relevant" to an agency's investigation at issue. The permissible scope of an administrative subpoena is, however, "variable in relation to the nature, purposes and scope of the inquiry."[19]

In order to satisfy the general reasonableness standard, the agency issuing the subpoena, in this instance the attorney general, must satisfy the court, in accordance with the *Powell* factors: (1) "the investigation will be conducted pursuant to a legitimate purpose," (2) "the inquiry may be relevant to the purpose," (3) "that the information sought is not already within the [agency's] possession," and (4) "the administrative steps required by the Code have been followed[.]" The courts have varied in their application of the last two factors, with some courts suggesting that the Supreme Court has obviated the requirement of considering these latter factors in decisions subsequent to *Powell.*[20]

17. *See* 18 U.S.C. § 3486(a)(1)(A)(i)(1).
18. 18 U.S.C. § 3486(a)(1)(B)(i)–(ii).
19. https://www.justice.gov/archive/olp/rpt_to_congress.htm
20. *Oklahoma Press Publ'g Co. v. Walling,* 327 U.S. 186, 209 (1946); United States v. Powell, 379 U.S. 48 (1964) (evaluating § 3486(a) healthcare offense subpoena authority and referring to standards established in United States v. Powell, 379 U.S. 48, 57–58 (1964)); *see, e.g.,* United States v. Bell, 564 F.2d 953, 959 (Temp. Emer. Ct. App. 1977) (last

Applicable enforcement mechanisms are also provided, in the event of noncompliance.

> In cases of refusal to comply with a subpoena, the Attorney General is authorized to seek the aid of a United States district court where the investigation is occurring or where the subpoenaed person resides. 18 U.S.C. §3486(c). Failure to obey a federal court's order to comply with a subpoena issued by the Attorney General under 18 U.S.C. § 3486(a) may be punished as contempt of court. 18 U.S.C. §3486(c). A district court's order requiring compliance with an administrative subpoena is generally treated as a final judgment under 28 U.S.C. § 1291, and, therefore, is immediately appealable.[21]

In sum, the United States does have the authority to reach covered entities, business associates, and subcontractors overseas. Lawyers should consult the U.S. Federal Rules of Civil Procedure, as well as complying with service requirements in the countries where the person is located.

## *Choice of Law Issues*

"The validity of a contractual choice-of-law clause is a threshold question that must be decided not under the law specified in the clause, but under the relevant forum's choice-of-law rules governing the effectiveness of such clauses."[22] A forum selection clause in a contract identifies the country, state, and/or type of court for purposes of litigation. This provision can also be included in an arbitration clause. In a choice-of-law clause, parties bargain for the designation of the jurisdiction and the law that will apply. For example, the parties may agree that an arbitration takes place in the London Court of Arbitration but the laws of India apply.

Terminology is important in the realm of contracts that have international consequences. First, "choice-of-law" is a term utilized by lawyers in the United States. In England, however, "the proper law of contract" is

---

two requirements too restrictive); United States v. Security State Bank & Trust, 473 F.2d 638, 641 (5th Cir. 1973) (governmental entity need only the two primary requirements).

21. Cobbledick v. United States, 309 U.S. 323, 330 (1940) (recognizing the immediate reviewable nature of a district court enforcement order).

22. Finance One Public Co. Ltd. v. Lehman Bros. Special Financing, Inc., 414 F.3d 325 (2005). *See* Case Headnote 5.

the equivalent and is not applied throughout Europe. As indicated in The Rome Convention on the Law of Applicable Contractual Obligations (1980), Art. 10, "applicable law" is used. In England, as Lord Wilberforce stated, "the law which governs the contract and the parties obligations under it; the law which determines normally its validity and legality, its construction and effect and the conditions of its discharge."[23] Hence, highlighting the importance of defining what the terms mean to avoid ambiguity down the line.

## *Contractual Jurisdiction in the Business Associate Agreement*

The Second Circuit's analysis in *Finance One Public Co. Ltd. v. Lehman Brothers Special Financing, Inc.* serves as a reminder of why forum, choice of law, and venue selection clauses are important, especially in the realm of business where international and healthcare data privacy and security laws overlap. Although a securities law case, it underscores the importance of identifying the choice of law. In this case, a Thai corporation brought suit against a Delaware corporation for breach of contract in relation to international derivative transactions. The Thai company, Finance One, had a principal place of business in Bangkok, and Lehman Brothers was a Delaware corporation with its principal place of business in New York.[24] The companies entered into an agreement in 1995 to execute Lehman Brothers' global derivative business.

Utilizing the industry association, International Swaps and Derivatives Association (ISDA)'s Master Agreement as a template, the parties addressed the choice-of-law clause and forum-selection clause, choosing New York as the governing law.[25] Lehman Brothers contended that an actual conflict is present only when the "choice of which to apply has been demonstrated to be 'outcome determinative.'"[26] The court rejected this notion, indicating that the differences need to be relevant to the issues and have a "significant *possible* effect on the outcome of trial."[27] In relation to the choice-of-law analysis, the court detailed the following:

---

23. Shipping Corp. v. Kuwait Ins. Co. [1984] AC 50, 55.
24. *Id.* at 327.
25. *Id.* at 328.
26. *Id.* at 331.
27. *Id.* (emphasis added).

> Determining which jurisdiction's law governs the scope of a valid choice-of-law clause is not a simple matter. On the one hand, once a court finds that a contractual choice-of-law clause is valid, the law selected in the clause dictates how the contract's provisions should be interpreted, and so arguably that law should also dictate how the choice-of-law clause—which is itself one of the contract's provisions—should be interpreted.[28]

The court also recognized that "set off claims" or claims that "arise out of different transactions" do not necessarily follow the same choice of law provisions.[29] Regarding New York's interpretation of choice-of-law analysis, the court distinguished between tort law and contract law.

> New York applies separate choice-of-law approaches to contract and to tort claims. In contract cases, New York courts apply "[t]he 'center of gravity' or 'grouping of contacts' choice of law theory. . . ." *Allstate Ins. Co.,* 597 N.Y.S.2d at 907, 613 N.E.2d 936. By contrast, "the preferred analytical tool in tort cases is to apply 'interest analysis,' where the policies underlying the competing laws are considered." *Id.* at 225, 597 N.Y.S.2d 904, 613 N.E.2d 936.[30]

Ultimately, the court applied Thai law to the set-off rights and found no violation of public policy.

---

28. *Id.* at 333. *See* Odin Shipping Ltd. v. Drive Ocean V MV, 221 F.3d 1348 (Table), 2000 WL 576436, at *1, 2001 U.S. App. LEXIS 11098, at *3 (9th Cir. May 11, 2000) (unpublished) ("The scope of [a choice-of-law] provision is a matter of contract construction and interpretation, however, which would in turn be governed by the law selected in the choice-of-law provision."). More commonly, however, courts consider the scope of a contractual choice-of-law clause to be a threshold question like the clause's validity. Courts therefore determine a choice-of-law clause's scope under the same law that governs the clause's validity-the law of the forum. *See, e.g.,* Krock v. Lipsay, 97 F.3d 640, 645 (2d Cir. 1996) (applying New York law to interpret scope of choice-of-law clause that selected Massachusetts law); Maltz v. Union Carbide Chems. & Plastics Co., 992 F. Supp. 286, 296 (S.D.N.Y.1998) (in diversity case transferred from Texas federal district court, applying Texas law to determine scope of choice-of-law clause that specified New York law); *cf.* Hodom v. Stearns, 32 A.D.2d 234, 301 N.Y.S.2d 146, 148 (App. Div. 4th Dep't 1969) (applying New York law to interpret scope of forum-selection clause specifying that suits under contract be brought in Oregon courts).

29. *Finance One,* 414 F.3d at 335.

30. *Id.* at 336.

This scenario could be equally applicable in any contractual agreement. Everything should be well thought out beforehand and specified. Paying attention to these details up front and making sure that the Master Service Agreement, Service Level Agreement, and Business Associate Agreement all coincide on these issues is crucial. Additionally, as addressed earlier, due diligence is required under the Omnibus Rule, and entities should make sure these items are addressed.

## *Service of Process*

According to Black's Law Dictionary, "service" is "1. [t]he formal delivery of a writ, summons, or other legal process. 2. The formal delivery of some other legal notice, such as a pleading."[31] Service is usually actual, but can take the form of constructive (i.e., another method), publication (i.e., newspaper), or substituted (i.e., mail). The type of acceptable service may be designated by law[32] or in a contract, such as a Master Service Agreement, Service Level Agreement, or a Business Associate Agreement. The

31. Black's Law Dictionary 648 (3d pocket ed. 2006).

32. *See* The Hague Service Convention. *See also* Cal. Ins. Code §§ 1610–1620. 1610. "Any of the acts described in Section 1611, when effected in this State, by mail or otherwise, by a foreign or alien insurer which is nonadmitted at the time of the solicitation, issuance or delivery by it of contracts of insurance to residents of, or to corporations authorized to do business in, this State, is equivalent to and shall constitute an appointment by such insurer of the commissioner and his successor or successors in office to be its true and lawful attorney, upon whom may be served all lawful process in any action, suit, or proceeding instituted by or on behalf of an insured or beneficiary arising out of any such contracts of insurance, and any such act shall be signification of its agreement that such service of process is of the same legal force and validity as personal service of process in this State upon such insurer.

1611. The acts referred to in Section 1610 are:

1. The issuance or delivery to residents of, or to corporations authorized to do business in, this State of contracts of insurance insuring (a) the lives or persons of residents of this State physically present herein at the time of such issuance or delivery or (b) property or operations located in this State.
2. The solicitation of applications for such contracts.
3. The collection of premiums, membership fees, assessments or other considerations for such contracts.
4. Any other transaction of business arising out of such contracts. 1612. Such service of process may be made as provided in Article 1 (commencing with Section 12919) of Chapter 2 of Division 3."

key is to keep the terms consistent, follow the U.S. Federal Rules of Civil Procedure, as well as any other country's laws regarding process.

When attempting to serve a party in a foreign country, in relation to HIPAA, here are some considerations:

- Where is the company's headquarters? For example, IBM is headquartered in Armonk, New York. It is also a multinational corporation with a multitude of offices worldwide.
- Where was the contract executed?
- Where did the violation, either technical or breach, occur?
- What other international laws are relevant?
- Does the country you are attempting to effect service in have legal procedures regarding service? Presuming that the entity is headquartered in another country and the PHI violation involves other countries' laws, then that country's substantive and procedural laws need to be addressed. A good place to start when assessing the types of acceptable service is the U.S. Department of State's (State Department's) website. A tool is available that allows the user to enter the desired country. From there, there are links to the following:
- International treaties and agreements
- Authentication of documents
- Service of process
- Obtaining evidence
- Enforcing judgments
- International judicial assistance. Because technology is global and one of the countries that is focused on is England, I typed in the United Kingdom. This step provided me with a short list of the following:
    - Party to Hague Service Convention? Yes
    - Party to Hague Evidence Convention? Yes
    - Party to Hague Apostille Convention? Yes
    - Party to Inter-American Convention? No
    - Service of Process by Mail? Yes

From this basic information, an attorney knows that service by mail is acceptable. From there, ascertain if a foreign government is involved. For the United Kingdom, for example, the Foreign Sovereign Immunities Act should be consulted.[33] This is important because many countries have a national health service, which may be a business associate or a

---

33. To avoid confusion and common mistakes, please take note of the following items before submitting a request for service under FSIA 1608(a)(4).

1. The defendant must be a foreign state or political subdivision, as defined in section 1603 of the Act, not an agency or instrumentality of a foreign state (to be served under section 1608(b) of the Act). The U.S. Department of State does not serve *natural persons* under the FSIA.
2. The Act allows for service under FSIA 1608(a)(4) only after *30 days have passed* since service was attempted under section 1608(a)(3) (by any form of mail requiring a signed receipt). The U.S. Postal service and private courier services can deliver documents to virtually any location. Plaintiffs should attempt service under FSIA 1608(a)(3) unless a foreign state has specifically objected to service by mail. To determine whether a particular country objects to service by mail, please see our country-specific judicial assistance information.
3. The documents must be *translated* into the official language of the foreign state to be served.
4. The summons sheet and the notice of suit should state a *60 day* (not 20 day) response time for the defendant.
5. The notice of suit (or default) should conform to the requirements of 22 CFR 93.2 (the statute specifically refers to notice of suit "in a form prescribed by the Secretary of State by regulation"). The notice of suit must contain a copy of the FSIA.
6. The Act requires plaintiff to have first attempted service under sections FSIA 1608(a)(1), (2) and (3) before proceeding to section 1608(a)(4). Thus, the U.S. Department of State requires a *statement in writing* from the plaintiff or the clerk certifying that these attempts were made or were otherwise not applicable.
7. There should be two copies of either (a) the summons, complaint and notice of suit or (b) a default judgment and notice of default (depending on the request).
8. In cases involving allegations of terrorism, plaintiffs should refer to section 1605A(a)(2)(iii) regarding arbitration requirements (however, we defer to the court as to the adequacy of any action taken by the plaintiffs in fulfillment of this requirement).
9. The Act requires the clerk of court dispatch the documents; however, a plaintiff may provide written confirmation that the court allowed plaintiff to act for the Clerk (after docketing).
10. All requests for FSIA 1608(a)(4) service of process should be addressed to: U.S. Department of State, CA/OCS/L, SA-17, 10th Floor, Washington, DC 20522-1710.
11. As of March July 3, 2010, the U.S. Department of State charges, in accordance with 22 CFR 22.1, a $2,275 fee (cashiers check/ money order should be made out to the U.S. Embassy or Consulate involved. For requests for service upon Iran and its political subdivisions the check or money order should be made out to "U.S. Embassy Bern).

Clerks who may have further questions regarding these issues may wish to refer to memos from the Administrative Office of U.S. Courts, dated, Nov. 7, 2000, May 20, 1982 and Nov. 6, 1980. The Federal District Court of the District of Columbia has also published an Attorney Manual for Service of Process on a Foreign Defendant, and the Federal

subcontractor of a U.S. corporation, especially when a U.S. covered entity has a location in the United Kingdom and its PHI is in the "cloud" and housed at a data center in London.

## The Importance of Mapping the HIPAA Security Rule to NIST and ISO

As business is global, so should HIPAA risk assessments or an equivalent cyber assessment. First, as Part II addresses, cybersecurity risk is a key area of focus across all facets of an organization—from the boardroom to the mail room. The most fundamental item a person can do is to conduct a HIPAA Risk Analysis, which maps the HIPAA Security Rule with NIST standards and ISO.

As stated on the HHS website,

> In February 2014, NIST released the Framework for Improving Critical Infrastructure Cybersecurity (Cybersecurity Framework) as directed in Executive Order 13636, Improving Critical Infrastructure Cybersecurity. The Cybersecurity Framework provides a voluntary, risk-based approach—based on existing standards, guidelines, and practices—to help organizations in any industry to understand, communicate, and manage cybersecurity risks. In the health care space, entities (covered entities and business associates) regulated by the Health Insurance Portability and Accountability Act (HIPAA) must comply with the HIPAA Security Rule to ensure the confidentiality, integrity, and availability of electronic protected health information (ePHI) that they create, receive, maintain, or transmit.[34]

This NIST-HIPAA crosswalk is something every assessment should consider when conducting a United States-only HIPAA risk analysis. What about when either a covered entity or business associate has international contractors or locations? Apart from HIPAA, as we learned

---

District Court for the Southern District of New York has created a publication, Foreign Mailing Instructions, both of which reference the Foreign Sovereign Immunities Act.

34. *HIPAA Security Rule Crosswalk to NIST Cybersecurity Framework,* U.S. Dep't of Health & Hum. Servs., https://www.hhs.gov/hipaa/for-professionals/security/nist-security-hipaa-crosswalk/index.html (last visited Apr. 15, 2023).

earlier in this book, the cybersecurity world also has the ISO 27001 standard, to describe security standards for an information security management system (ISMS).[35] By mapping HIPAA to ISO 27001, organizations can better protect their valuable intellectual property and other sensitive data, including PHI.[36]

ISO 27001 has 114 security controls, and at least 47 can be leveraged to comply with HIPAA requirements.[37] Five HIPAA requirements, which can be mapped to ISO 27001 control objectives are included in the following chart.[38]

| **Five HIPAA to ISO Mapping Items** |
|---|
| HIPAA Requirement 164.308(a)(2) Assigned Security Responsibility to ISO 27001 Control: A.6.1.1 Information Security Roles and Responsibilities |
| HIPAA Requirement 164.308(a)(5) Security Awareness and Training to ISO 27001 Control: A.7.2.2 Information Security Awareness, Education, and Training |
| HIPAA Requirement 164.310(b) Workstation Use to ISO 27001 Control: A.8.1.3 Acceptable Use of Assets |
| HIPAA Requirement 164.308(a)(4) Information Access Management to ISO 27001: A.9.1 Business Requirements of Access Control and A.9.2 User Access Management |
| HIPAA Requirement 164.312(a)(1) Access Control (to Information Systems) to ISO 27001:<br>A.9.4 System and Application Access Control. For HIPAA and ISO, this relates to controlling access systems and applications, as well as implementing technical access controls, which are set forth in policies and procedures and include information access restriction, secure log-on procedures, password management system, role-based access, and access control to any program source code. |

The best approach is to map HIPAA, NIST, and ISO to achieve the maximum benefit. It is imperative to include the items that do not overlap, as well as those that do.

## Looking Forward to the Next Horizon

As cybersecurity threats evolve, so will technology and the cyber risk and compliance landscape. Looking ahead, counsel for covered entities and

35. *See* https://reciprocity.com/blog/how-to-map-hipaa-to-iso-27001/ (last visited Apr. 15, 2023).

36. *Id.*

37. *Id.*

38. *Id.*

business associates alike should consider, on an international scale, the following trends: (1) data poaching;[39] (2) reproductive health privacy;[40] (3) biometrics;[41] and (4) cybersecurity risk implications for boards, including insurance.[42] Being proactive is more important than ever moving forward, as well as adopting a prevention, detection, and correction approach when cultivating a culture of compliance. In sum, cyber risk and cybersecurity is here to stay, especially in the healthcare sector. As we look to the next horizon, it is important to keep the fundamentals described herein and in *What Are . . . International HIPAA Considerations?* and build upon them.

39. *See* https://www.jdsupra.com/post/contentViewerEmbed.aspx?fid=fa61411a-b98e-467d-a2fd-d78d3f9c8539 (last visited Apr. 15, 2023) (indicating that "85% of the mobile apps fail to explain to users how their personal data is being collected, stored or handled").

40. Press Release, The White House, FACT SHEET: Biden-Harris Administration Announces Actions to Protect Patient Privacy at the Third Meeting of the Task Force on Reproductive Healthcare Access (Apr. 12, 2023), https://www.whitehouse.gov/briefing-room/statements-releases/2023/04/12/fact-sheet-biden-harris-administration-announces-actions-to-protect-patient-privacy-at-the-third-meeting-of-the-task-force-on-reproductive-healthcare-access/; https://www.ohchr.org/sites/default/files/Documents/Publications/NHRIHandbook.pdf (last visited Apr. 15, 2023).

41. *See* https://pro.bloomberglaw.com/brief/biometric-data-privacy-laws-and-lawsuits/ (last visited Apr. 15, 2023).

42. *Comments on the Cybersecurity Risk Management, Strategy, Governance, and Incident Disclosure – Release No. 33-11038; 34-94382; IC-34-529*, SEC, https://www.sec.gov/comments/s7-09-22/s70922.htm (last visited Feb. 27, 2023).

# CHAPTER 10

# Looking Ahead

This notion of all of a sudden everything has changed is true of both cybersecurity and artificial intelligence (AI). The three key areas that healthcare sector participants, as well as those persons that engage in businesses involving consumers' individually identifiable health information (IIHI) are AI, the potential liability of chief information security officers (CISO) and boards of directors, and the focus on healthcare as critical infrastructure. It is with an eye toward the future that this last chapter is written.

## Artificial Intelligence

There is a difference between traditional AI and generative AI. "Generative AI and Traditional AI lies in their objectives and functioning. While Traditional AI aims to perform specific tasks based on predefined rules and patterns, Generative AI goes beyond this limitation and strives to create entirely new data that resembles human-created content."[1] NIST defines "AI" in two ways:

1. A branch of computer science devoted to developing data processing systems that performs functions normally associated with human intelligence, such as reasoning, learning, and self-improvement.
2. The capability of a device to perform functions that are normally associated with human intelligence such as reasoning, learning, and self-improvement.[2]

---

1. *See* Pavan Vadapalli, *Generative AI vs Traditional AI: Understanding the Differences and Advantages,* UPGRAD, https://www.upgrad.com/blog/generative-ai-vs-traditional-ai/# (last visited Nov. 11, 2023); *see also What Is Generative AI?,* IBM, https://research.ibm.com/blog/what-is-generative-AI# (last updated Aug. 15, 2023) (stating that "[g]enerative AI refers to deep-learning models that can generate high-quality text, images, and other content based on the data they were trained on").

2. *See* https://csrc.nist.gov/topics/technologies/artificial-intelligence (last visited Nov. 11, 2023).

In order to provide guidance to organizations "designing, developing, deploying or using AI systems to help manage the many risks of AI technologies" NIST published its *Artificial Intelligence Risk Management Framework* (AI RMF 1.0). Analogous to the NIST Cybersecurity Framework 2.0, a core component is governance (see Figure 10.1).[3]

**Figure 10.1** AI Risk Management Framework

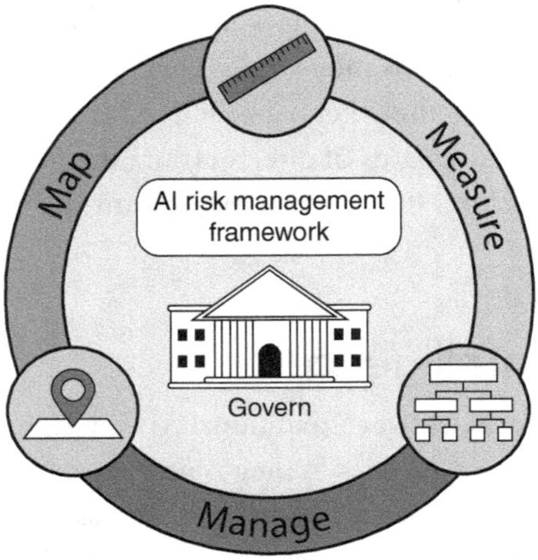


Credit: N. Hanacek/NIST

As directed by the National Artificial Intelligence Initiative Act of 2020,[4] *the goal of the AI RMF is to offer a resource to the organizations designing, developing, deploying, or using AI systems to help manage the many risks of AI and promote trustworthy and responsible development and use of AI systems.* With the concepts of "Map, Measure, and Manage," along with the overarching factor of governance, in mind, recent government factors should also be considered and integrated into a risk mitigation and compliance plan. In October 2022, the White House Office of Science and Technology (OST) published *The Blueprint for an AI Bill of Rights: Making Automated Systems Work for the American People* (AI BoR).[5] The AI

3. *AI Risk Management Framework*, NIST, https://www.nist.gov/itl/ai-risk-management-framework (last visited Nov. 11, 2023).

4. Pub. L. No. 116-283 (Jan. 1, 2021) (emphasis added).

5. *See* https://www.whitehouse.gov/wp-content/uploads/2022/10/Blueprint-for-an-AI-Bill-of-Rights.pdf (Oct. 2022).

BoR has five principles: (1) safety and effectiveness; (2) *algorithmic discrimination protections*; (3) *data privacy*; (4) notice and explanations; and (5) human alternatives, consideration, and feedback.[6] Building on the AI BoR, on October 30, 2023, the White House issued an Executive Order (EO)—*Safe, Secure, and Trustworthy Development and Use of Artificial Intelligence*,[7] followed by *OMB Releases Implementation Guidance Following President Biden's Executive Order on Artificial Intelligence* on November 1, 2023.[8] The EO "establishes new standards for AI safety and security, protects Americans' privacy, advances equity and civil rights, stands up for consumers and workers, promotes innovation and competition, advances American leadership around the world, and more."[9] The EO expressly refers to NIST, as well as addressing potential threats to critical infrastructure and cybersecurity risks.[10]

In particular, sections 4.1 and 4.2 of the EO—*Ensuring the Safety and Security of AI*—stood out because it dovetails into Health Insurance Portability and Accountability Act (HIPAA) Security Rule fundamentals, General Data Protection Regulation (GDPR) requirements, the EU AI Act, cybercriminal utilization of AI, and patient safety in relation to critical infrastructure. Sections 4.1 and 4.2 expressly state:[11]

> 4.1. Developing Guidelines, Standards, and Best Practices for AI Safety and Security.
>
> > (a) Within 270 days of the date of this order, to help ensure the development of safe, secure, and trustworthy AI systems,

---

6. *Id.* at 9–11 (emphasis added).

7. Press Release, The White House, FACT SHEET: President Biden Issues Executive Order on Safe, Secure, and Trustworthy Artificial Intelligence (Oct. 30, 2023), https://www.whitehouse.gov/briefing-room/statements-releases/2023/10/30/fact-sheet-president-biden-issues-executive-order-on-safe-secure-and-trustworthy-artificial-intelligence/.

8. Press Release, The White House, OMB Releases Implementation Guidance Following President Biden's Executive Order on Artificial Intelligence (Nov. 1, 2023), https://www.whitehouse.gov/omb/briefing-room/2023/11/01/omb-releases-implementation-guidance-following-president-bidens-executive-order-on-artificial-intelligence/.

9. Press Release, *supra* note 7.

10. *Id.*

11. Press Release, The White House, Executive Order on the Safe, Secure, and Trustworthy Development and Use of Artificial Intelligence (Oct. 30, 2023), https://www.whitehouse.gov/briefing-room/presidential-actions/2023/10/30/executive-order-on-the-safe-secure-and-trustworthy-development-and-use-of-artificial-intelligence/.

the Secretary of Commerce, acting through the Director of the National Institute of Standards and Technology (NIST), in coordination with the Secretary of Energy, the Secretary of Homeland Security, and the heads of other relevant agencies as the Secretary of Commerce may deem appropriate, shall:

(i) Establish guidelines and best practices, with the aim of promoting consensus industry standards, for developing and deploying safe, secure, and trustworthy AI systems, including:

(A) developing a companion resource to the AI Risk Management Framework, NIST AI 100-1, for generative AI;

(B) developing a companion resource to the Secure Software Development Framework to incorporate secure development practices for generative AI and for dual-use foundation models; and

(C) launching an initiative to create guidance and benchmarks for evaluating and auditing AI capabilities, with a focus on capabilities through which AI could cause harm, such as in the areas of cybersecurity and biosecurity.

(ii) Establish appropriate guidelines (except for AI used as a component of a national security system), including appropriate procedures and processes, to enable developers of AI, especially of dual-use foundation models, to conduct AI red-teaming tests to enable deployment of safe, secure, and trustworthy systems. These efforts shall include:

(A) coordinating or developing guidelines related to assessing and managing the safety, security, and trustworthiness of dual-use foundation models; and

(B) in coordination with the Secretary of Energy and the Director of the National Science Foundation

(NSF), developing and helping to ensure the availability of testing environments, such as testbeds, to support the development of safe, secure, and trustworthy AI technologies, as well as to support the design, development, and deployment of associated PETs, consistent with section 9(b) of this order.

(b) Within 270 days of the date of this order, to understand and mitigate AI security risks, the Secretary of Energy, in coordination with the heads of other Sector Risk Management Agencies (SRMAs) as the Secretary of Energy may deem appropriate, shall develop and, to the extent permitted by law and available appropriations, implement a plan for developing the Department of Energy's AI model evaluation tools and AI testbeds. The Secretary shall undertake this work using existing solutions where possible, and shall develop these tools and AI testbeds to be capable of assessing near-term extrapolations of AI systems' capabilities. At a minimum, the Secretary shall develop tools to evaluate AI capabilities to generate outputs that may represent nuclear, nonproliferation, biological, chemical, critical infrastructure, and energy-security threats or hazards. The Secretary shall do this work solely for the purposes of guarding against these threats, and shall also develop model guardrails that reduce such risks. The Secretary shall, as appropriate, consult with private AI laboratories, academia, civil society, and third-party evaluators, and shall use existing solutions.

4.2. Ensuring Safe and Reliable AI. (a) Within 90 days of the date of this order, to ensure and verify the continuous availability of safe, reliable, and effective AI in accordance with the Defense Production Act, as amended, 50 U.S.C. 4501 *et seq.*, including for the national defense and the protection of critical infrastructure, the Secretary of Commerce shall require:

(i) Companies developing or demonstrating an intent to develop potential dual-use foundation models to provide the Federal Government, on an ongoing basis, with information, reports, or records regarding the following:

(A) any ongoing or planned activities related to training, developing, or producing dual-use foundation models, including the physical and cybersecurity protections taken to assure the integrity of that training process against sophisticated threats;

(B) the ownership and possession of the model weights of any dual-use foundation models, and the physical and cybersecurity measures taken to protect those model weights; and

(C) the results of any developed dual-use foundation model's performance in relevant AI red-team testing based on guidance developed by NIST pursuant to subsection 4.1(a)(ii) of this section, and a description of any associated measures the company has taken to meet safety objectives, such as mitigations to improve performance on these red-team tests and strengthen overall model security. Prior to the development of guidance on red-team testing standards by NIST pursuant to subsection 4.1(a)(ii) of this section, this description shall include the results of any red-team testing that the company has conducted relating to lowering the barrier to entry for the development, acquisition, and use of biological weapons by non-state actors; the discovery of software vulnerabilities and development of associated exploits; the use of software or tools to influence real or virtual events; the possibility for self-replication or propagation; and associated measures to meet safety objectives; and

(ii) Companies, individuals, or other organizations or entities that acquire, develop, or possess a potential large-scale computing cluster to report any such acquisition, development, or possession, including the existence and location of these clusters and the amount of total computing power available in each cluster.

Overall, when developing or utilizing AI, users must ensure that AI applications "are safe, secure, and trustworthy."[12] Around the same time, the World Health Organization outlined items for regulation of AI for health.[13]

There are six main objectives related to AI, which notably mention GDPR and HIPAA. Specifically,

- To foster trust, the publication stresses the importance of **transparency and documentation**, such as through documenting the entire product life cycle and tracking development processes.
- For **risk management**, issues like "intended use," "continuous learning," human interventions, training models, and cybersecurity threats must all be comprehensively addressed, with models made as simple as possible.
- Externally **validating data** and being clear about the **intended use** of AI helps ensure safety and facilitate regulation.
- A commitment to **data quality**, such as through rigorously evaluating systems pre-release, is vital to ensuring systems do not amplify biases and errors.
- The challenges posed by important, complex regulations—such as GDPR in Europe and HIPAA in the United States of America—are addressed with an emphasis on understanding the scope of jurisdiction and consent requirements, in service of **privacy and data protection**.
- Fostering **collaboration** between regulatory bodies, patients, healthcare professionals, industry representatives, and government partners can help ensure products and services stay compliant with regulation throughout their life cycles.[14]

Perhaps not surprisingly, the World Health Organization (WHO) considerations mirror those of the United States—appreciating that AI is complex and that nondiscrimination, as well as data quality, privacy, and security.

---

12. Press Release, *supra* note 7.

13. *WHO Outlines Considerations for Regulation of Artificial Intelligence for Health*, WHO (Oct. 19, 2023), https://www.who.int/news/item/19-10-2023-who-outlines-considerations-for-regulation-of-artificial-intelligence-for-health.

14. *Id.*

## *SolarWinds*: Board of Director and Executive Liability Considerations

On August 4, 2023, the U.S. Securities and Exchange Commission (SEC) published its cybersecurity final rule, with an effective date for most items of September 5, 2023. The final rule applies to national registrants, foreign private issuers, and business development companies.[15] As the SEC highlights,[16]

> The new rules add Item 1.05 to Form 8-K. Item 1.05 requires disclosure of the following information regarding a material cybersecurity incident:
>
> - The material aspects of the nature, scope, and timing of the incident; and
> - The material impact or reasonably likely material impact on the registrant, including on the registrant's financial condition and results of operations.
>
> Item 1.05 does not require the registrant to disclose specific or technical information about its planned response to the incident or its cybersecurity systems, related networks and devices, or potential system vulnerabilities in such detail that would impede its response or remediation of the incident.
>
> Importantly, the deadline for filing an Item 1.05 Form 8-K is tied not to discovery but to the registrant's determination that the incident is material. The filing must be made within four business days of the registrant determining that a cybersecurity incident is material. The rule instructs registrants to make the materiality determination "without unreasonable delay." As is the case in other securities contexts, information is material if "there is a substantial likelihood that a reasonable shareholder would consider it important"[17] in making an investment decision, or if it would have "significantly altered the 'total mix' of

15. 88 Fed. Reg. 51896 (Aug. 4, 2023).

16. *Cybersecurity Risk Management, Strategy, Governance, and Incident Disclosure,* SEC, https://www.sec.gov/corpfin/secg-cybersecurity (last updated Nov. 14, 2023).

17. *Id.* (citing TSC Indus. v. Northway, 426 U.S. 438, 449 (1976); Matrixx Initiatives v. Siracusano, 563 U.S. 27, 38–40 (2011); and Basic v. Levinson, 485 U.S. 224, 240 (1988)).

> information made available."[18] Because materiality's focus is on the total mix of information from the perspective of a reasonable investor, registrants assessing the materiality of a cybersecurity incident should do so through the lens of the reasonable investor. Their evaluation should take into consideration all relevant facts and circumstances, which may involve consideration of both quantitative and qualitative factors.

In light of this, the SEC's October 30, 2023, complaint against SolarWinds Corp. (SolarWinds) and Timothy Brown, its CISO underscores the increased focus of the SEC on both cybersecurity and individual liability for cybersecurity executives.[19] In its complaint, the SEC alleges that investors were defrauded through a series of material "misstatements, omissions, and schemes that concealed both the Company's poor cybersecurity practices and its heightened—and increasing—cybersecurity risks."[20] In essence, what was happening behind the scenes and what was relayed to the market told two very different stories.[21] As the U.S. Government Accountability Office (GAO) recounted,[22]

> Beginning in September 2019, a campaign of cyberattacks, now identified to be perpetrated by the Russian Foreign Intelligence Service (hereafter referred to as the threat actor), breached the computing networks at SolarWinds—a Texas-based network management software company. The threat actor first conducted a "dry run," injecting test code into SolarWinds' network management and monitoring suite of products called Orion. Then, beginning in February 2020, the threat actor injected trojanized (hidden) code into a file that was later included in SolarWinds' Orion software updates. SolarWinds released the software

18. *Id. See also* Rule 405 under the Securities Act of 1933 (Securities Act), 17 C.F.R. § 230.405, and Exchange Act Rule 12b-2, 17 C.F.R. § 240.12b-2, (defining "material").

19. Securities & Exch. Comm'n v. SolarWinds Corp. & Timothy G. Brown, Case No. 23-cv-9518 (S.D.N.Y. Oct. 30, 2023), https://www.sec.gov/files/litigation/complaints/2023/comp-pr2023-227.pdf.

20. *Id.* at 1.

21. *Id.*

22. *SolarWinds Cyberattack Demands Significant Federal and Private-Sector Response*, GAO (Apr. 22, 2021), https://www.gao.gov/blog/solarwinds-cyberattack-demands-significant-federal-and-private-sector-response-infographic.

updates to its customers not realizing that the updates were compromised. The trojanized code had provided the threat actor with a "backdoor"—a program that can give an intruder remote access to an infected computer. According to cybersecurity researchers, the threat actor was then able to remotely exploit the networks and systems of SolarWinds' customers who had downloaded the compromised software updates using a sophisticated computing infrastructure.

Since SolarWinds is widely used in the federal government to monitor network activity on federal systems, this incident allowed the threat actor to breach infected agency information systems. SolarWinds estimates that nearly 18,000 of its customers received a compromised software update. Of those, the threat actor targeted a smaller subset of high-value customers, including the federal government, to exploit for the primary purpose of espionage.[23]

The SEC set forth three types of public disclosures, which were allegedly "materially false and misleading statements and omissions" and include the following:

a. Statements that purported to describe the Company's cybersecurity practices and policies, including "Security Statement" posted to the Company's website throughout the Relevant Period [October 2018 through at least January 12, 2021];
b. Form S-1 and S-8 Registration Statements and periodic reports filed with the SEC throughout the Relevant Period; and
c. A Form 8-K filed with the SEC on December 14, 2020 regarding the massive SUNBURST cybersecurity incident that impacted SolarWinds' Orion software platform.[24]

The complaint goes on to give specific examples of the three categories of alleged violations, which include substandard technical, administrative, and physical safeguards, as required by NIST SP 800-53 rev. 4.[25] For example,

23. *Id.*
24. *Id.* at 3.
25. *Id.* at 15–17.

> Despite the claim in its Security Statement that it followed the NIST Framework, in multiple internal assessments between 2019 and 2021, SolarWinds met only a small fraction of the cybersecurity controls laid out in the NIST Framework and had "no program/practice in place" for the majority of the controls, as Brown and SolarWinds knew, or were reckless or negligent in not knowing.[26]

As Reuters published, "[t]he heart of the SEC's complaint is that SolarWinds was selling a perception of security that the substance of their security program could not back up. More bluntly, that SolarWinds lied about their security program and security measures in place."[27]

Subsequently, SolarWinds posted a response, which as any litigator appreciates is a bold move when there is active litigation. In sum, SolarWinds vehemently states that the "SEC's lawsuit is fundamentally flawed—legally and factually—and we plan to defend vigorously against the charges."[28] In sum, despite the text messages, emails, audits, and other documents, SolarWinds "categorically den[ies] those allegations. The company had appropriate cybersecurity controls in place before SUNBURST."[29] This lawsuit comes on the heels of the conviction and sentencing of Uber's former chief security officer for covering up a data breach and lying to executives at Uber and various federal government agents.[30]

Having adequate cybersecurity compliance and making misstatements to both the market and the government are areas that are only going to continue to be a focus both in the United States and abroad. Given that healthcare is internationally considered critical infrastructure, lawsuits by private attorneys and government agencies, as well as government enforcement actions, are likely.

---

26. *Id.* at 16.

27. John Bandler, *SolarWinds and the SEC Lawsuit,* REUTERS (Nov. 21, 2023), https://www.reuters.com/legal/legalindustry/solarwinds-sec-lawsuit-2023-11-21/.

28. SolarWinds, *Setting the Record Straight on the SEC and SUNBURST,* ORANGEMATTER (Nov. 8, 2023), https://orangematter.solarwinds.com/2023/11/08/setting-the-record-straight-on-the-sec-and-sunburst/.

29. *Id.*

30. Press Release, DOJ, Former Chief Security Officer of Uber Sentenced to Three Years' Probation for Covering Up Data Breach involving Millions of Uber User Records (May 5, 2023), https://www.justice.gov/usao-ndca/pr/former-chief-security-officer-uber-sentenced-three-years-probation-covering-data.

## Healthcare as Critical Infrastructure

The third area to continue to watch are sectors that are considered critical infrastructure. The U.S. Cybersecurity & Infrastructure Security Agency (CISA) identified other complimentary sectors—energy, agriculture, communications, and so on—as being interdependent with healthcare.[31] "The Healthcare and Public Health Sector relies on collaboration to protect all sectors of the economy from hazards such as terrorism, infectious disease outbreaks, and natural disasters."[32] The healthcare sector is one of the top targets for cyberattacks.

Similar to the United States, ENISA, the European Union Agency for Cybersecurity, recognizes that healthcare is considered critical infrastructure.[33]

> Since 2014, ENISA has been working closely with the cybersecurity community for healthcare across the EU to foster the security and resilience of the sector by supporting the development and implementation of a relevant policy and regulatory framework, by raising awareness, publishing guidelines and good practices, facilitating information sharing and more. The complexity and diversity of the sector requires that all stakeholders such as hospitals and other health services operators, national authorities, manufacturers and health IT professionals work together and contribute.[34]

ENISA continues to issue reports, and, in its latest report, it summed up the notion that "the concept of investment also extends to the human element."[35]

---

31. *Healthcare and Public Health Sector,* CISA, https://www.cisa.gov/topics/critical-infrastructure-security-and-resilience/critical-infrastructure-sectors/healthcare-and-public-health-sector (last visited Nov. 21, 2023).

32. *Id.*

33. *ENISA Is Working towards a Cyber Secure and Resilient Health Sector in the EU,* ENISA, https://www.enisa.europa.eu/topics/critical-information-infrastructures-and-services/health (last visited Nov. 21, 2023).

34. *Id.*

35. *Cybersecurity Investment: Spotlight on Vulnerability Management,* ENISA (Nov. 16, 2023), https://www.enisa.europa.eu/news/cybersecurity-investment-spotlight-on-vulnerability-management.

# INDEX